ALSO BY DAVID KESSLER

The Needs of the Dying

Visions, Trips, and Crowded Rooms

You Can Heal Your Heart (coauthor with Louise Hay)

On Grief & Grieving (coauthor with Elisabeth Kübler-Ross)

Life Lessons (coauthor with Elisabeth Kübler-Ross)

Finding Meaning

The SIXTH STAGE of GRIEF

DAVID KESSLER

Written with support of the Elisabeth Kübler-Ross Family
and the Elisabeth Kübler-Ross Foundation

SCRIBNER

New York   London   Toronto   Sydney   New Delhi

Scribner

An Imprint of Simon & Schuster, Inc.

1230 Avenue of the Americas

New York, NY 10020

First Scribner hardcover edition November 2019

SCRIBNER and design are registered trademarks of The Gale Group, Inc.,
used under license by Simon & Schuster, Inc., the publisher of this work.

For information about special discounts for bulk purchases,
please contact Simon & Schuster Special Sales at 1-866-506-1949
or business@simonandschuster.com.

The Simon & Schuster Speakers Bureau can bring authors to your live event.
For more information or to book an event, contact the Simon & Schuster Speakers
Bureau at 1-866-248-3049 or visit our website at www.simonspeakers.com.

Manufactured in the United States of America

1 3 5 7 9 10 8 6 4 2

Library of Congress Control Number: 2019028917

ISBN 978-1-5011-9273-9
ISBN 978-1-5011-9275-3 (ebook)

*To my son in heaven and
my son on earth*

Contents

III. Meaning

Author's Note

The stories in this book recount the challenges that numerous families and their friends have faced in grief and the insights they have gained. The names and other characteristics of many of the people in these stories have been changed. Some of the people portrayed in these pages are composites of two or more individuals.

Finding
Meaning

❈

Introduction

In 1969, Elisabeth Kübler-Ross identified the five stages of dying in her groundbreaking book *On Death and Dying*. As a psychiatrist, she saw that patients who were dying appeared to go through common experiences or stages. Her work captured the world's attention and would forever change the way we talk and think about death and dying. She ushered the truth of this universal experience out of shadowy euphemism and into the light.

Decades later, I was privileged to have been her protégé and friend, and to have coauthored with her a book entitled *Life Lessons: Two Experts on Death & Dying Teach Us About the Mysteries of Life and Living*. In the second book we wrote together, *On Grief and Grieving*, which was her last, Elisabeth asked me to help adapt the stages she had observed in the dying to account for the similar stages we had also observed in those who are grieving. The five stages of grief are:

Denial: shock and disbelief that the loss has occurred

Anger: that someone we love is no longer here

Bargaining: all the what-ifs and regrets

Depression: sadness from the loss

Acceptance: acknowledging the reality of the loss

The five stages were never intended to be prescriptive, and this holds true for both dying and the subject of this book, grieving. They are not a method for tucking messy emotions into neat packages. They don't prescribe, they describe. And they describe only a general process. Each person grieves in his or her own unique way. Nonetheless, the grieving process does tend to unfold in stages similar to what we described, and most people who have gone through it will recognize them. In the years since that book's publication, I've experienced a great loss myself, and I can confirm that the five stages really do capture the feelings we experience as we grapple with the death of loved ones.

The fifth of Kübler-Ross's five stages is acceptance. At this stage, we acknowledge the reality of the loss. We take some time to stop and breathe into the undeniable fact that our loved ones are gone. There's nothing easy about this stage. It can be extremely painful, and acceptance doesn't mean that we are okay with the loss, or that the grieving process is now officially over. However, there's been an assumed finality about this fifth stage that Elisabeth and I never intended. Over the years I came to realize that there's a crucial sixth stage to the healing process: meaning. This isn't some arbitrary or mandatory step, but one that many people intuitively know to take and others will find helpful.

In this sixth stage we acknowledge that although for most of us grief will lessen in intensity over time, it will never end. But if we allow ourselves to move fully into this crucial and profound sixth stage—meaning—it will allow us to transform grief into something else, something rich and fulfilling.

Through meaning, we can find more than pain. When a loved one dies, or when we experience any kind of serious loss—the end of a marriage, the closing of the company where we work, the destruction of our home in a natural disaster—we want more than the hard fact of that loss. We want to find meaning. Loss can wound and paralyze. It can hang over us for years. But finding meaning in loss empowers us to find a path forward. Meaning helps us make sense of grief, as you will see from the many stories in this book from people who have gone through this sixth stage.

When working with people whose loved ones have died, I often see how hard they search for meaning. It doesn't matter whether the death occurred after a long debilitating illness or if it came as a total shock after an accident or anything else that was sudden and unexpected. There's often a desire to see meaning in it.

What does meaning look like? It can take many shapes, such as finding gratitude for the time they had with loved ones, or finding ways to commemorate and honor loved ones, or realizing the brevity and value of life and making that the springboard into some kind of major shift or change.

Those who are able to find meaning tend to have a much easier time grieving than those who don't. They're less likely to remain stuck in one of the five stages. For those who do get stuck, this can manifest in many different ways, including sudden weight gain (or loss), drug or alcohol addiction, unresolved anger, or an inability to form or commit to a new relationship out of fear of experiencing yet another loss. If they remain stuck in loss, then they may become consumed by it, making *it* the focus of their life to the point where they lose all other sense of purpose and direction. Although you can't pin all of your troubles or vices on getting stuck after a loss, there is almost always a connection.

Grief is extremely powerful. It's easy to get stuck in your pain and remain bitter, angry, or depressed. Grief grabs your heart and doesn't seem to let go.

But if you can manage to find meaning in even the most senseless loss, you can do more than get unstuck. When circumstances are at their worst, you can find your best. You can keep growing and finding ways to live a good and someday even a joyous life, one enriched by the lessons and love of the person who died.

The search for meaning after loss will lead each of us along divergent paths. Candy Lightner famously founded Mothers Against Drunk Driving (MADD) in 1980 after her daughter, Cari, was killed by a repeat drunk-driving offender. Even though she never understood why her daughter had to die, she was able to find great meaning in forming a group that saved the lives of others. For her, nothing was worth the cost of losing her daughter, but the ability to create something good from that death helped give her the sense that her daughter's life as well as her own had meaning.

John Walsh started the TV show *America's Most Wanted* after the murder of his son, Adam. He found great purpose in fighting to get criminals off the streets so no other children would be harmed.

Walsh and Lightner found meaning in starting national organizations. Most of us are not going to act on such a large scale, but that's not an obstacle to creating meaning. We can find meaning in the smallest of moments if we look for it and make a point of creating it.

Marcy grew up with a father whose favorite TV personalities were Milton Berle, Danny Thomas, and Morey Amsterdam. Because her father told her he had met Danny Thomas once, a memory he cherished, after he died she thought of him anytime she saw or heard any reference to Danny Thomas.

One day she was in line at the post office to mail a package and buy some stamps.

"What kind of stamps would you like?" the postal worker asked.

"Forever stamps."

"We have flags and flowers and commemorative stamps. Do you want to see them?"

"Who cares?" Marcy thought. "They all do the same thing." But she decided to look at what they had. Out came a vast array of stamps, and suddenly Marcy noticed a Danny Thomas stamp. Thinking of her father, she bought many sheets of the stamps. She didn't frame them or do anything special with them. She just used them. Now, whenever she's mailing a letter or paying a bill and she reaches for a stamp, she sees Danny Thomas and smiles. In those little moments, memories of her father's life come back to her and bring her comfort. She doesn't need anything more than a moment of sweet remembrance to find meaning in the life of her father.

In my work with grieving people, I've often been asked, "Where am I trying to find meaning? The death? The loss? The event? The life of the person I loved? Or am I trying to find meaning in my own life after the loss?"

My answer is yes, yes, yes, yes, and yes. You may find meaning in all of those, which will lead you to deeper questions and deeper answers. Maybe your meaning will come by finding rituals that commemorate your loved one's life, or by offering some kind of contribution that will honor that person. Or the loss of your loved one may cause you to deepen your connection to those who are still with you, or to invite back into your life people from whom you've been estranged. Or it may give you a heightened sense of the beauty of the life we are all so privileged to have as long as we remain on this earth.

Deirdre's husband had died two years before the events she recounted to me, and she still missed him deeply. They had had a very close, loving marriage, the loss of which left a large hole in her life. Her father had lost his brother the month before the death of Deirdre's husband. She and her father had bonded in their grief. She said, "I knew his pain. He loved his brother. I got it."

Deirdre and her family live in Hawaii, and on the day she later described to me they had gathered at a campground near Pearl Harbor to watch a canoe race in which her niece was participating. A few minutes before the race was supposed to start, a nuclear warning siren pierced the morning air. Simultaneously, a text alert on Deirdre's phone read *Inbound missile alert. This is not a drill.*

"A group of people came out from under a pavilion where the coaches were meeting," Dierdre later told me. "They announced over the PA system, 'Okay, everybody be safe, get home safely, and make sure everyone's got a ride.'" She continued:

My dad, brother, uncle, and the rest of the family started breaking down their tents. I went to get my dad's ropes from the car, and when I came back, everyone was gone, even my mom.

"Bye," I said. "But where's Mom?" Then I saw her in her car. She was rushing home, too. I went to see my dad, who was the only one who hadn't left yet. He didn't seem to be in a hurry and I asked, "Are you okay?"

Why did everybody else just take off? Why didn't they stay to say goodbye? It seemed ridiculous. If we were going to die, why not be together with those we loved when it happened? If there had actually been an inbound missile, everyone would have died while they were in their cars racing home. No one said *I love you* or *hope we see each other again*. No one shared any final memories. We are a close family. Usually.

It was interesting to me that unlike everyone else, the two people who felt no need to run were my dad and me. We made a decision to be together in the time we had left. We had an amazing discussion during that terrifying period, and I thanked him for being my dad. He thanked me for being his daughter. We talked about what we loved most about life.

As a psychologist, I have tried to analyze why Dad and I stayed together for what we thought would be our last moments while everyone else in our family fled. I think it's because the deaths of people we had been so close to had taught us about how valuable life is. If we only had five or ten minutes to live, we didn't want to squander them.

It turned out to be a false alarm, but I love how Dad and I made a decision to spend what remained of our lives doing something meaningful. None of us know how long we have. Five minutes, five years, or fifty years. We don't have that kind of control, but we do have control over how we choose to spend whatever time remains to us.

Ultimately, meaning comes through finding a way to sustain your love for the person after their death while you're moving forward with your life. That doesn't mean you'll stop missing the one you loved, but it does mean that you will experience a heightened awareness of how precious life is, as Deirdre did. Whenever it ends—at a few days or in extreme old age—we rarely think that life is long enough. Therefore we must try to value it every day and live it to the fullest. In that way we do the best honor to those whose deaths we grieve.

Here are some thoughts that may guide you in understanding meaning:

1. Meaning is relative and personal.
2. Meaning takes time. You may not find it until months or even years after loss.
3. Meaning doesn't require understanding. It's not necessary to understand why someone died in order to find meaning.
4. Even when you do find meaning, you won't feel it was worth the cost of what you lost.
5. Your loss is not a test, a lesson, something to handle, a gift, or a blessing. Loss is simply what happens to you in life. Meaning is what *you* make happen.
6. Only you can find your own meaning.
7. Meaningful connections will heal painful memories.

When I began writing this book, I had spent decades writing, teaching, and working with those in grief. I was well into my fifties by then and considered myself to be deeply acquainted with grief, not just as a professional, but also in my private life. Anyone who has reached that age will have experienced grief. Both my parents had died, along with a nephew who was like my brother. However, nothing in either my personal or my professional life as a grief specialist had prepared me for the loss I experienced when I embarked on this book—the unexpected death of my twenty-one-year-old son. This was a loss so shattering that despite all the years I'd spent helping others through their grief, I didn't know if there was anything that could assist me through my own. And despite my awareness that the search for meaning is one of the keys to healing from grief, I did not know if there was any way I could find meaning in this loss. Like so many others who grieve, something in me felt that *my* grief was too great to be healed.

In the year 2000, I had adopted two wonderful boys from the Los Angeles County foster care system. David was four years old and his brother, Richard, was five. By that time the two of them had been in five different foster homes and had one failed adoption. Addiction in their family background had hindered their permanent placement, as had the fact that David had been born with drugs in his system. When I heard that, I feared that it might mean something was wrong with him that would not be fixable. But it only took looking at the faces of those two little boys to tell me that love conquers all. The adoption went through, and in the years that followed, my belief in the power of love appeared to be confirmed. David and Richard both made an amazing turnaround and were wonderful kids.

Unfortunately, the trauma of David's younger years came back to haunt him when he became a teenager. At around seventeen, David began experimenting with drugs. Luckily, he came to me not long afterward and told me he was addicted and needed help. In the next few years, our lives were filled with rehab and twelve-step programs. By the time he was twenty, however, he was sober, in love with a wonderful woman who was a recent social work graduate, and entering his first year in college. David had shown a real interest in following a career in medicine, yet had gone back and forth on what kind of career—or whether he should be developing an interest in something else, and yet I felt hopeful. But then a few days after his twenty-first birthday, he made some typical relationship mistakes and he and his girlfriend broke up. That was when he met up with a friend from rehab who was also having a tough time and they used drugs again. The friend lived. David died.

I was across the country on a lecture tour when I received a call from Richard, sobbing that his brother was dead. In the months that followed, I was in an agony of grief. Fortunately,

I was surrounded by friends and family who saw me not as a grief expert, but as a father who had to bury his son.

In the early days after losing David, amazing people like my partner, Paul Denniston, and spiritual teacher Marianne Williamson, one of the godmothers for my sons, spent countless hours with me, listening, talking, trying to help in any way they could. My friend Diane Gray, who headed the Elisabeth Kübler-Ross Foundation at the time and is a bereaved parent herself, told me, "I know you're drowning. You'll keep sinking for a while, but there will come a point when you'll hit bottom. Then you'll have a decision to make. Do you stay there or push off and start to rise again?"

What she said felt true. I knew in that moment that I was still in the deep end of the ocean, and I also knew that I was going to have to stay there for a while. I wasn't ready to surface. But even then, I felt I would continue to live, not only for the sake of my surviving son but for my own sake as well. I refused to allow David's death to be meaningless or to make my life meaningless. I had no idea what I would do to wrest meaning from this terrible time. For the moment, all I could do was to go through Kübler-Ross's stages and allow them to unfold as slowly as I needed. Still, I knew I couldn't and wouldn't stop at acceptance. There had to be something more.

At first I was not able to find any consolation in memories of my love for my son. I had a lot of anger at that time—at the world, at God, and at David himself. But in order to go on, I knew I would have to find meaning in the grief I was feeling. In my deep sorrow, I thought about a quote I share at my lectures: grief is optional in this lifetime. Yes, it's true. You don't have to experience grief, but you can only avoid it by avoiding love. Love and grief are inextricably intertwined.

As Erich Fromm says, "To spare oneself from grief at all costs can be achieved only at the price of total detachment, which excludes the ability to experience happiness."

Love and grief come as a package deal. If you love, you will one day know sorrow. I realized I could have skipped the pain of losing David if I'd never known and loved him. What a loss that would have been. In the moment when I really began to understand that, I found gratitude for my son having come into my life and for all the years I got to spend with him. They weren't nearly long enough, but they had changed and enriched my life immeasurably. That was the beginning of my being able to see something meaningful in my grief.

As time goes by, I have been able to keep finding deeper meaning in David's life as well as in his death, as I will describe in later chapters. Meaning is the love I feel for my son. Meaning is the way I have chosen to bear witness to the gifts he gave me. Meaning is what I have tried to do to keep others from dying of the same thing that killed David. For all of us, meaning is a reflection of the love we have for those we have lost. Meaning is the sixth stage of grief, the stage where the healing often resides.

In the immediate aftermath of my son's death, I wasn't sure if I would ever write again, lecture again, or even want to live again. I canceled everything for six weeks. But then I felt I needed to get back to work. I needed to be of service and keep my own pain moving. As hard as my son's death was, I still wanted to live in the face of devastating loss. I knew that David would want me to live fully.

Writing this book has been part of my return to life. When I began, I wasn't sure if I believed my own words about finding meaning in the face of life-altering grief. I had been in such deep pain that I didn't know if meaning was possible after such a shattering loss. But it has turned out that in exploring the search for meaning in the devastation of loss, I have discovered that meaning is both possible and necessary. I hope that *Finding Meaning: The Sixth Stage of Grief* will be a boon for anyone who's struggling to figure out how to live after a loss. I hope that reading it will be as healing for others as writing it has been for me.

PART I

Every Loss Has Meaning

CHAPTER ONE

What Is Meaning?

Birds sing after a storm; why shouldn't people feel as
free to delight in whatever sunlight remains to them?
—Rose Kennedy

In 1975, my mentor and coauthor, Elisabeth Kübler-Ross, said,
"Death does not need to be a catastrophic, destructive thing:
indeed, it can be viewed as one of the most constructive positive and creative elements of culture and life." Most of us do
not experience it that way.

At one of my lectures, I asked my audience, "Who has been
with a loved one at the moment of death?" Many hands went
up. I picked one and asked him what his experience had been.
He said that his father's death was the most traumatic thing
that ever happened to him and that he was still overwhelmed
by it. The next person said, "My father died also. That moment
was one of the most meaningful experiences our family ever
shared."

Both men had lost a father they loved, both had grieved
deeply. But one man had experienced the death as something
meaningful and had moved forward; the other had found no
meaning in the experience, only trauma.

We essentially die in the same way, but one family can see it
as meaningful and the other as traumatic. Grief is the experience and natural feelings that come with loss. Some deaths are
traumatic when they are accompanied by exposure to the loved
one's physical agony, medical procedures, suddenness—as in

a death by suicide or homicide, motor vehicle accident, natural disaster, other catastrophic situation—violence, and many other factors that shape our experience of loss. Trauma always has grief mixed in, but not all grief is traumatic.

There are many factors in how we experience death and grief: age (both our own and that of the person who died), whether the death was expected, and how the person died. There are also many factors involved in how we move forward—or don't. The person who sees death as sacred has found a way to find meaning in it. To those who get mired in a seemingly endless slog of grief, death feels utterly devoid of meaning. But it doesn't have to be that way, even when we're faced with the most terrible kinds of loss and suffering. Viktor Frankl's cornerstone work, *Man's Search for Meaning*, is a beacon for those who wonder how meaning can emerge from tragedy. His insight was born out of the years he spent in Nazi concentration camps. Frankl wrote that each of us has the ability to choose how we respond to even the most terrible of circumstances. "We who have lived in concentration camps can remember the men who walked through the huts comforting others, giving away their last piece of bread. They may have been few in number, but they offer sufficient proof that everything can be taken from a man but one thing: the last of the human freedoms—to choose one's attitude in any given set of circumstances, to choose one's own way." Frankl suggested that when we are faced with a situation that is hopeless, unchangeable, "we are challenged to change ourselves." When we make the choice to do that, we can turn tragedy into an occasion for growth.

Frankl's work shed light on suffering—on how life's most challenging moments can produce amazing resilience, courage, and creativity. I spoke about this to a mother whose child had died. "I don't care about Frankl," she said. "He lived. His suffering ended with a new life, and mine ended in death. There is no meaning."

Though I believe that the potential for meaning is ever present in our lives, I also understood that pushing her to accept it would have been a violation. It was too soon for her to see any light in her pain. But there will come a point, after she has honored the grief, when she will want to stop hurting. The yearning will be too much. The emptiness will become too encompassing. I'm not talking about lessening her connection to her loved one, but rather decreasing the suffering associated with the connection. In that pain, that opening, she can begin to explore how to find meaning.

The grieving mind finds no hope after loss. But when you're ready to hope again, you will be able to find it. Bad days don't have to be your eternal destiny. That doesn't mean your grief will get smaller over time. It means that you must get bigger. As the saying goes, "No mud, no lotus." The most beautiful flower grows out of the mud. Our worst moments can be the seeds of our best moments. They have an amazing power to transform us.

A decade after Elisabeth Kübler-Ross's assertion that positives could be found in loss and death, psychologist Christopher Davis and his colleagues wrote an article in the American Psychological Association's *Journal of Personality and Social Psychology* in which they asserted that having *any* understanding of meaning was preferable to having none, and that the content of that understanding did not seem to matter. Some people will find meaning in belief in afterlife. Others will find meaning in the memories of their loved ones. Still others will find meaning in simply being able to be present for their loved ones' last hours. Pain, death, and loss never feel good, but they're unavoidable in our lifetime. Yet the reality is posttraumatic growth happens more than posttraumatic stress. That is consistent with what I've seen in my work with those who are grieving and also my work with the dying in palliative care and hospice. Wherever you find it, meaning matters, and meaning heals.

Early Losses

When people ask me what I do, I pause. Do I tell them that I write books about death and grief and lecture around the world? Or that I have worked in palliative care and hospice for decades? That I have a master's degree in bioethics and help people decide when enough is enough in medical care? When it is time to consider hospice or palliative care? Do I explain that I'm a specialist police reserve officer on a trauma team, as well as serving as a member of a Red Cross disaster team? Or that I trained for a pilot's license and have taken part in helping those whose loved ones died in two aviation disasters? Unlike my mentor, Elisabeth Kübler-Ross, who mostly worked with death in a hospital setting, I'm trained as a modern-day thanatologist. In other words, I don't deal with death only in the hospital or hospice, but also at crime scenes and plane crashes. I follow grief wherever it takes me, which usually brings me to scenes of death and dying, but it can also lead me to divorce and other kinds of losses.

The list of my activities and affiliations may sound like a strange, incoherent mishmash. But the truth is that although I am a hybrid of all those things, there is an underlying theme uniting them all. When I look back on my reasons for following this unusual path, I see that my career choices weren't random. It was my destiny to become who I am because of what happened to me during the course of a few days when I was thirteen years old.

My mother battled health problems throughout much of my childhood. On New Year's Eve 1972, I walked into her bedroom, gave her a kiss, and said, "Mom, 1973 will be the year you get better." Within days, she underwent severe kidney failure and was transferred from our local hospital to one in New Orleans that was larger and better equipped.

Mom was put in an intensive care unit that allowed visitors to see their family members for only ten minutes every two hours. My father and I spent most of our time sitting in the hospital lobby waiting for those brief, precious visits, hoping for a sign that she was getting better and could go home. Since my father had no money for a hotel, we also had to sleep in that waiting room.

There was not much close to the hospital, no mall or stores, nothing else to see. In fact, the only thing around was the hotel across the street where we could not afford to stay. But boredom is boredom. Since we had to be close to the hospital and that hotel at least offered us the possibility of a change of scene, we spent many hours sitting in that lobby, too. That was life: Mom was in the hospital and we were hanging out in hospital and hotel lobbies.

One day when we were at the hotel, there was a sudden eruption of activity, and someone yelled, "Fire!" Everyone began running outside because there was a fire on the eighteenth floor. Flames appeared on the balcony and the fire department and police arrived quickly. Then the unthinkable happened. As the firefighters climbed the ladder to fight the fire, shooting began. This was not just a fire—it was a massacre. The man who had set the fire was now on top of the building, taking aim at people with a gun.

Within seconds, police were everywhere while people rushed into the adjoining buildings for cover. It was scary stuff for a child who had been sitting in the hospital for days on end facing another terrifying thing—the serious illness of his mother. The siege went on for thirteen hours and resulted in seven deaths, including three police officers. It is now considered one of the first mass shootings in the United States. Today you can see it on YouTube if you search for New Orleans Sniper 1973.

During the two days that followed, my mother stopped talking and I knew she was getting sicker. But seeing her was a challenge since there was a rule that you had to be fourteen years old to visit a patient and I was only thirteen. Although most of the nurses were lenient and allowed me to go into her room, some wouldn't. One nurse even told me to come back when I was fourteen!

Three days after the shooting, Dad and I were told that my mom didn't have long to live, and unfortunately the next day it was the "Rule Nurse" who was on duty. She refused to let me see my mother, or to ease up on the ten-minutes-every-two-hours regulation. Therefore, my mother died alone that day. That's the way things happened back then. Families, especially children, were often not allowed to be present during a patient's final moments. When they were, it was only at the mercy of the caregivers.

At the end of that painful day, I went on my first plane ride. My father and I were flying to Boston to arrange for my mother's funeral. Since they knew I had just lost my mother, the pilots wanted to give a sad kid a little fun. As a well-meaning gesture they invited me into the cockpit to "help" them fly the plane. Although the captain told me I was flying it, I of course never really had control of the plane, but as a child I believed that I did—and I was terrified. I remember looking out from the cockpit, feeling lost and overwhelmed, and thinking I was going to make a mistake and crash the plane. Luckily, all 148 passengers made it through my first "solo."

Now I see how all the things I do in my professional life—dealing with death in the medical world, working in end-of-life ethics, becoming a specialist reserve police officer, learning to fly a plane, and working with the Red Cross on aviation disasters—are attempts to regain some of the control I felt I lost when my mother died. And through these choices I found a healing process that gave meaning to my own life and offered me an opportunity to use what I learned to help others. I've become someone who could have helped that young boy who was in so much distress. My career is living proof that we teach what we need to learn.

But that is not the end of this story.

To this day, New Orleans will always be a city with lots of meaning for me because it's where my mother died. I've been back many times, and during some of those visits, I've stood outside the hospital where she died and looked across the street at the Howard Johnson's hotel where my father and I had whiled away so many hours between visits to my mother. In 2005, the hospital was devastated by Hurricane Katrina and it was deemed too damaged and old to rebuild. There was a plan to tear it down and build a new modern hospital not far from there.

In 2015, I embarked on a one-year lecture tour that took me to the US, the UK, and Australia. The lecture company that booked my US tour chose the cities and venues, and it wasn't surprising that New Orleans was one of the cities in which I would be lecturing. The bookers always make it easy for me, putting me in the same hotel where I am scheduled to speak. As I was looking over my New Orleans itinerary, I saw that I'd be speaking at the Holiday Inn Superdome Hotel. When I Googled the hotel's address, I discovered, to my shock, that it was the same hotel where the fire and the sniper attack had occurred decades earlier. It had undergone a major renovation and had a new name, but it was the same place.

When I told my lecture company the story, they said, "We'd be happy to move you to another venue. We don't want you to be uncomfortable."

"No," I said. "I think it's a full-circle moment of meaning for me." I had decided that staying there was something I should do. Healing doesn't mean the loss didn't happen. It means that it no longer controls us.

As the date got closer, my past began to demand more of my attention. I wondered what had been built on the site of the old hospital where my mother had died. After a quick search on the Internet, I found out that although the new hospital was about to open, the old one was apparently still standing.

Wanting to see it, I called the hospital administration in New Orleans. A manager told me that the hospital was indeed still there, but it had been condemned and entry was forbidden. I told her my story and asked, "Is there any way I could get into the closed hospital?"

"No," she said quickly. "Because of Katrina, there might be mold and it isn't safe."

"What about with an escort, a hard hat, and a mask?"

"I don't think so."

"I understand," I told her. "But would you be willing to inquire for me? It would mean so much to me."

An hour later, she called back. "I'm not sure what did it, your story or maybe they were familiar with your work, but they said yes. The head of security for the hospital system will meet you there Sunday, the day before your lecture, and escort you into the lobby. But you can only see the lobby."

I was suddenly thirteen years old again. How ironic, I thought, that all these years later I was still restricted to the lobby. At least now, as an adult, I understood why.

When I got to the hospital on Sunday afternoon, I was surprised by the kindness of the security director. "When I heard your story," he said, "I did a little research with some of the old-timers. The ICU where your mother would have been is on the sixth floor west. Would you like to go there?"

"Yes, absolutely."

"The building has minimal electricity, so the elevators aren't running," he said. "But we could walk up to the tenth floor, cross buildings, and walk down to the sixth floor."

Before I knew it, we were on the tenth floor of the old hospital. Ceiling tile lay on the floor, dislodged light fixtures swayed above us, abandoned patient rooms were empty, and everything—beds, equipment, chairs—had been removed.

As we walked down to the ninth floor, we passed abandoned nursing stations and more empty rooms, and I couldn't help but think about all the lives that had passed through there. Finally we arrived at the sixth-floor ICU. Whatever else may have changed, the ICU entrance double doors were the same, and decades later, I could still recognize them.

I turned to the security director and said, "These are the doors I wasn't allowed to go past."

"Now you can," he said. "Go ahead."

As I began to push the door open, I turned to him and said, "Her bed was the second on the left." When I entered the unit, I looked at the space where my mother's bed would have been.

Just above it, there was a call light that was flashing green. I froze. We had walked through four floors of patients' rooms and hadn't seen one call light blinking.

My skeptical mind said it was a random light left on in an abandoned building. Or perhaps the police chief had turned it on because he knew where my mother died. But as soon as I thought this, I realized what a stretch it was. How could he possibly have known that this was the room where she died? I hadn't told him my mother's full name, and even if I had, he would have had to pull records from decades ago in an abandoned hospital. Medical records are usually destroyed after seven years.

What did the green light mean? We often talk about "meaning making." Life offers us layers of meaning. We make of them what we will. What meaning did I give to this green light? What meaning did it have on its own? A green light often means it's okay to go. At that moment it meant I was finally able to go to the place where my mother died. But the green light they often use in doctors' offices has another meaning. Once a patient is brought to an examination room, a green light outside the room means that there is a patient waiting to be seen. Was the green light telling me that my mother was waiting to be seen— by me? Could she somehow have known I was coming and wanted to give me a sign that she was there? If this place was such a power spot for me, would it be a power spot for her, too?

Standing in that room, I thought about my friend Louise Hay, who told me, "We arrive in the middle of the movie and we leave in the middle of the movie." We included that in our book *You Can Heal Your Heart*. We have finite time on this earth. I had grown from a young boy questioning why my mother had to die, into a man who was healed. That thirteen-year-old boy could never have imagined that one day he would be standing at the exact same spot where his mother had taken her last breath forty-two years earlier. Now I was about the same age as my mother when she died, and being there made me feel whole at last. I was no longer a victim, but rather a victor over my loss. I could remember my mother with more love than pain. I found great meaning in knowing that I had turned my loss into a vocation that helps thousands survive the worst moments of their lives.

Meaning Making

Gail Bowden's child Branden was born with spina bifida. He had to use a catheter to go to the bathroom, wear braces on his legs, and use a wheelchair. Yet Gail was determined to give him a great life. Thanks to Gail, Branden grew up happy. He loved the color yellow, and he took a liking to cars, especially yellow Volkswagen Beetles. Before long, he had quite an extensive toy car collection.

When Branden was seventeen, Gail walked into his room one day and found him unresponsive. He was transported to the hospital and the doctor gave Gail the heartbreaking news that Branden would never wake up. He said that her son was essentially dead, and she might consider donating his healthy organs.

Although she could scarcely process what was happening, she agreed to the donation. If they couldn't save Branden's life, at least he would get to save other lives. Without realizing it, Gail was seeking meaning in her son's life and death. She sat with her son as they removed his breathing tube and he quietly died. It was very peaceful, and Gail believed that he returned home to heaven.

A few years later, just after Gail's other son, Bryan, went off to summer camp, they moved into a new home. Gail was unpacking boxes when she heard a knock at the door. She had arranged for a worker to come and paint the new apartment, using Branden's favorite color, yellow.

"Hi, I'm Ken, the painter," the man said.

"You're a week early," Gail told him.

"My first job in the area was canceled," Ken replied, "so the company sent me over early."

"Everything is still in boxes," she told him. "I was hoping

to organize things before you came, but since you're here, you might as well go ahead and start."

Ken began painting while Gail continued to unpack. "Do you live alone?" he asked her.

"My son Bryan is in camp."

"Do you have any other kids?"

Gail had dealt with the awkwardness of that question before. Sometimes she talked about Branden, but other times she said, "It's just Bryan and me." For some reason, this time the question caught her off guard and she stood there, startled, wondering what to say. "I had another son named Branden who died at seventeen," she said.

"I'm so stupid," Ken replied. "I always stick my foot in my mouth. So sorry for asking."

"It's okay," she told him, and he continued to paint. After a few minutes, Ken said, "I'm sorry about your son. I know what it's like to be very sick. I almost died four years ago at the age of forty-two, but my life was saved by a kidney transplant. I just celebrated my four-year transplant anniversary last month."

"When did you have your transplant?"

"February."

"February what?"

"February 13, 2008," he said. "I'll never forget the date."

"Branden died on February 12, 2008."

"What a coincidence," Ken said. "My donor was a twenty-one-year-old man who died in a car accident."

Gail continued packing and Ken went back to painting. After a little while, Gail went out to run an errand, leaving Ken alone in her apartment with one wall painted yellow. When she returned, she found him standing right where she had left him, staring into space. He hadn't made any progress.

"Is there something wrong?" Gail asked.

"I lied to you."

"You're not a painter?"

"No, not about that. I have Branden's kidney."

"What?"

"When you told me that Branden was your son's name and you were Gail, I realized that I'd received a letter from you after I had the transplant. I was given the option to write back to you and I'm so ashamed that I never did."

Stunned, Gail picked up the phone and called the transplant center. She told the counselor, "I hired a painter and he told me that he has Branden's kidney. How can we be sure?"

The transplant counselor said, "The odds of that occurring would be almost impossible, but give me his name."

Gail asked Ken his full name and gave it to the counselor. He reviewed the confidential file and confirmed that Ken had indeed received one of Branden's kidneys. Gail began to cry when she heard this. Ken was equally shocked by the unlikely connection that had been made. Gail found enormous meaning in knowing that her son's kidney was in this living, breathing man. When Bryan got home from camp and heard what happened, he said, "It's as if Branden found his way home, Mom."

In the midst of her loss, Gail had accepted the tragedy in front of her. She made meaning of her son's life by deciding to donate his organs, determined that Branden would live on by saving the lives of others. Now she had met one of those whom he'd saved. Later, when Gail met Ken's wife and kids, she realized how much his children had needed him. They had been in dire straits. Not only had Branden's kidney saved Ken's life, but it had had a dramatic impact on his family.

You may be thinking that Gail lived in a small town and it wasn't such a remarkable coincidence that Ken ended up as her painter. Even if that were true, the odds against her discovering that he had her son's kidney were long. Consider these possibilities:

- Gail might not have mentioned her son, Branden.
- Ken might not have mentioned his kidney transplant.
- Gail might have painted the room herself and never met Ken.
- Gail might have hired a different company.

- The company might have sent a different painter.
- If Ken had come at his scheduled time, Gail might not have been as available to talk.

You may still think that these are just some fortunate coincidences, but the reality is that Gail doesn't live in a small town. She lives in Buffalo, New York, where there are eighteen hundred painters to choose from. In the end, it doesn't matter whether the odds of Gail's meeting Ken were long or short. To Gail it felt as though it was meant to happen, a validation of everything she had done. When she had donated Branden's organs, she had decided that something good was going to come out of the bad. Meeting Ken, she was able to see that good in action. Today Gail works with other families as they go through the organ donation/transplant process. In helping others make some of the toughest decisions, she continues to create meaning from Branden's life.

Can All of Us Create Meaning?

What about those who can't find meaning? Is it possible that the ability to find or make meaning is inherent in our DNA? Do some of us get it and others not? In other words, are only some of us born to make lemonade out of the lemons of tragedy? The answer is no. Finding meaning is for everyone.

Jane had a hard time finding meaning after a devastating series of losses. Her little boy had died of a rare cancer, and from everything she told me about him, he'd been a lively, mischievous child who even at his young age had made many friends. Sitting in front of me, unable to meet my eyes, she whispered, "After our child died, we got divorced. I have no one now. There isn't any meaning here. What meaning can there possibly be in my child, Tommy, dying at two years old?"

"More than you can imagine," I said. "Your child has meaning. I now know Tommy. He will forever live in my heart, and that's just the beginning. Meaning can be found in the life of anyone who has ever occupied space on this planet or in someone's heart. It is there if you look for it."

I asked Jane if I could share a story about Linda, a friend of mine.

Linda was nine years old when her mother died of cancer. She felt robbed of a normal life, jealous of all her classmates with their perfect mom-and-dad families. During summer break, when she was twelve, she went with her father on a business trip to Massachusetts. On their first night, after dinner they decided to take a walk. As they strolled through the charming old city where they were staying, they saw a small cemetery off one of the main streets and decided to explore it.

Soon Linda came across a tombstone that was engraved with the name and dates William Berkley, March 15, 1802–March 18, 1802. "This baby died after three days," she said to her father. "That's all he got, three days!"

Her father told her that baby deaths happened much more often then than they do now. Until that moment, Linda had never thought about others' losses because she had been so focused on her own. "I never realized I could have had Mom for even less time." For the first time in her life she felt a brief sense of gratitude for the years she had been able to share with her mother. But unfortunately, the gratitude was short lived, because it gave way to a pang of fear.

"What if you died?" she asked her father.

"Honey, let's hope that doesn't happen for a long time."

She told him she had seen a commercial on TV that said, "What would you do if a loved one died and you didn't have the money to bury them?" The ad promised life insurance policies for only a one dollar a month, and she wanted her father to buy one. She had overheard the discussions he'd had about having to borrow money to pay for her mother's funeral.

"Linda, I'll do my best when my time comes to make sure things are covered." He saw her pained face and said, "Would you feel better knowing I got one of those one-dollar-a-month policies?"

"Yes," she said. "But don't die!"

He kissed her forehead and said, "Okay, I won't, at least not for a long time. I'll get that policy for you."

That was one of the first times they'd had an honest discussion about life-and-death matters, but it would not be the last. Luckily, Linda's father lived for many decades, and during those years they grew ever closer. At the time of his death at age eighty-four, Linda was married with two children and had become a successful media specialist for an online TV network. She gave her father a beautiful send-off and buried him in the same cemetery as her mother.

About six weeks later, Linda rushed home early from work one night to get ready for a cancer charity auction that her TV network was sponsoring. She grabbed her mail and found an envelope from Freedom Mutual Life Insurance. Opening it she discovered a check for six hundred dollars. She suddenly realized that it was from the policy her dad had bought after they saw the baby's tombstone. The irony of this check did not escape her. She no longer needed the money and she had no clue what to do with it. But she hoped she could find some way of using it that would honor her father.

That evening, when Linda and her husband were at the fund-raiser, they watched video clips that her TV network had produced about the good work the charity was doing to help so many in need. The head of the charity explained that that night was the culmination of their fund-raising and they were hoping to achieve their goal of raising half a million dollars, which a donor would match dollar for dollar and give them another half million.

Toward the end of the evening, Linda and her husband decided to sneak away a few minutes early. They said their goodbyes and were making their way out when Linda heard the MC talking about their fund-raising goal for the night. The amount raised had been tallied, $499,400. They were $600 short of reaching their goal.

Linda was suddenly electrified. Without having to think

twice, she knew this was what she would do with the money from her father's life insurance. She immediately raised her hand and said, "Six hundred dollars here!"

The emcee turned to her and said, "Done! We reached our goal. Thank you. You just put us over the top and we doubled our money. One million dollars raised!"

Looking back at that moment, Linda was astonished to realize that a child who had lived for only three days in 1802 had not only had a powerful effect on her own twelve-year-old self, helping her to realize how lucky she had been to have her mother with her for nine years, but would now be able to touch countless others. It brought home to her that no life, however brief, is without meaning.

"That's quite a story," Jane said.

I touched Jane's hand. "Remember how I told you that if you occupy space on the planet, you have meaning? Think of all the meaning in that story. That child who died in 1802 had meaning for his parents. And then nearly two centuries later he had meaning for a little girl still mourning her mother. Now, two hundred and fourteen years after he died, there was still more meaning to be found in his brief life. Who knows how many lives will be affected by the million dollars they raised that night thanks to Linda's donation, which itself was a product of the exchange she had had with her father at the child's grave?"

"I guess I only thought of my child's life having meaning," Jane said as we talked that day. "I never thought of his death having meaning."

"Meaning is all around us," I said. "We just have to look to discover it."

Like Jane, many people assume there is no meaning in loss. It's true that sometimes we have to search long and hard for it or get help from another to find it. But it's there if we look. All of us get broken in some way. What matters is how we get up and put the pieces back together again.

CHAPTER TWO

Grief Must Be Witnessed

For the dead and the living, we must bear witness.
—Elie Wiesel

Each person's grief is as unique as their fingerprint. But what everyone has in common is that no matter how they grieve, they share a need for their grief to be witnessed. That doesn't mean needing someone to try to lessen it or reframe it for them. The need is for someone to be fully present to the magnitude of their loss without trying to point out the silver lining.

This need is hardwired in us, since our emotions bind us to one another, and in those bonds is the key to our survival. From the moment we're born, we realize we're not alone. Our brains are equipped with mirroring neurons, which is why when the mother smiles, the baby smiles back. This continues into adulthood. I remember walking down the street one day and a man said to me, "Howdy." I'm not usually someone who says "Howdy." But I instinctively said back to him, "Howdy!" This is more than copying each other's expressions. It's also about the emotions underlying the expressions. The mirroring neurons enable mother and child to pick up on each other's emotions.

Dr. Edward Tronick is part of a psychology team that made a short video that shows what happens if babies do not feel their emotions reflected and acknowledged by those around them. First we see a ten-month-old sitting in a high chair, eyes wide and happily fixed on his mother's smiling face. The baby and mother mirror each other as I described above. One laughs, then the other laughs; the baby points and the mother looks in the direction in which he's pointing. But then at the direction of the researchers, the mother turns away, and when she turns back to the baby, she has a blank look on her face. The confused baby does everything to try to get a reaction out of her. He cries and screams in distress. This is an innate reaction, because children know on a subconscious level that they need others for survival. If their survival is dependent on someone who is unable to be truly present for them, they suffer.

The same is true for adults. If they are grieving, they need to feel their grief acknowledged and reflected by others. But in our hyperbusy world, grief has been minimized and sanitized. You get three days off work after a loved one dies and then everyone expects you to carry on like nothing happened. There are fewer and fewer opportunities for those around you to bear witness to your pain, and this can be very isolating.

I was touring in Australia when I met a researcher who told me about the work she was doing to study the way of life in the northern indigenous villages of Australia. One of the villagers told her that the night someone dies, everyone in the village moves a piece of furniture or something else into their yard. The next day, when the bereaved family wakes up and looks outside, they see that *everything has changed* since their loved one died—not just for them but for everyone. That's how these communities witness, and mirror, grief. They are showing in a tangible way that someone's death matters. The loss is made visible.

In this country, too, it was once common for us to come together as a community to bear witness to the grief experienced when a loved one died. But in our current culture, the mourner is made to feel that though his or her own world has been shattered, everyone else's world goes on as if *nothing* has changed. There are too few rituals to commemorate mourning, and too little time allotted to it.

Grief should unite us. It is a universal experience. If I'm talking to someone with a physical ailment, I can listen and empathize, but I may never have that particular problem. When I'm with someone whose loved one died, however, I know I'll be in their shoes someday and I try to understand what they are feeling. Not to change it—just to acknowledge it fully. I feel privileged when someone shares their pain and grief with me. The act of witnessing someone's vulnerability can bring the person out of isolation if the witnessing is done without judgment.

Too often outsiders who may have the best of intentions will suggest to a bereaved person that it's time to move on, embrace life, and let go of grief. But grief should be a no-judgment zone. Those who understand what you're going through will never judge you or think your grief is out of proportion or too prolonged. Grief is what's going on inside of us, while mourning is what we do on the outside. The internal work of grief is a process, a journey. It does not have prescribed dimensions and it does not end on a certain date.

When people ask me how long they're going to grieve, I ask them, "How long will your loved one be dead? That's how long. I don't mean you'll be in pain forever. But you will never forget that person, never be able to fill the unique hole that has been left in your heart. There is what I call the one-year myth— we should be done and complete with all grieving in one year. Not remotely true. In the first year of your loss, you're likely to mourn and grieve intensely. After that, your grief will probably fluctuate. It will seem to lessen, then something will trigger it, and you'll find yourself back in the full pain of loss. In time it will hurt less often and with less intensity. But it will always be there."

That's about as specific as I can get in answering the question. As vague as it is, it still doesn't cover all the possibilities. Over many years of grief work, I've come to realize that if I've seen *one* person in grief, I've only seen that *one* person in grief. I can't compare one griever to another, even if they're in the same family. One sister cries a lot and the other one doesn't. One son is vulnerable and raw. The other just wants to move on. Some people are expressive. Others shy away from their feelings. Some have more feelings. Some have less. Some are more productive and practical in their grieving style. They have a "buckle down and move on" mentality. We can mistakenly think that people who show no visible signs of pain should be in a grief group, getting in touch with and sharing their feelings. But if that is not their style in life, it won't be in grief, either. They must experience loss in their own way. Suggesting otherwise will not be helpful to them.

The Light and Dark of Grief

In our modern world, our grief is often witnessed online. When I post quotes about grief on social media, I notice different kinds of responses. If I post hopeful, optimistic quotes about healing, they give hope to many people, but don't resonate with others. Those who are in a dark place aren't ready to hear about hope, often because they're at the beginning of the grieving process and their grief is too acute to allow for any other emotions. They just want the darkness of their grief to be seen and acknowledged. Their tears are evidence of their love, proof that the person who died was someone who mattered deeply. If I post something like, "Today it feels like the pain will never end," or "Grief feels like a dark cloud that encompasses the whole sky," that will resonate with them. It mirrors and validates their feelings, which can be far more consoling than trying to find something positive in the situation.

Some grieve with darkness, some with light, some with both, depending on where they are in the cycle of grief. It would be a mistake to conclude that one is better than the other or that there's a right way to grieve. There are just different ways to grieve, different feelings evoked by loss. This is also true of our relationship to hope. Hope can be like oxygen to people in grief. For others, however, especially in the early stages, it can feel invalidating. "In my sorrow, how dare you want me to feel hopeful . . . about what? Do you need me to hope to make *you* feel more comfortable?"

Hope has a very close relationship with meaning. In the same way our meaning changes, so does hope. Sometimes when I work with someone stuck in grief, I will say, "It sounds like hope died with your loved one. It seems all is lost."

Surprisingly they perk up. "Yes, that's it."

They feel witnessed. I often say, "A loved one's death is permanent, and that is so heartbreaking. But I believe your loss of hope can be temporary. Until you can find it, I'll hold it for you. I have hope for you. I don't want to invalidate your feelings as they are, but I also don't want to give death any more power than it already has. Death ends a life, but not our relationship, our love, or our hope."

Sometimes I meet someone in grief who tells me that a family member or friend said something terrible—which often turns out to be some variation of "time heals all" or "be happy your loved one is at peace now." Such statements can make the bereaved think that their feelings have not been witnessed. Most of us want to say something helpful, but we may not realize that our timing and delivery are off. If the griever needs to remain in a dark place for a while, then trying to offer some kind of cheer will be very hurtful. We must really *see* the person we are trying to comfort. Loss can become more meaningful— and more bearable—when reflected, and reflected accurately, in another's eyes.

We also have to remember that our own thoughts about the one who died are irrelevant. Maybe we think our friend's mother was so awful that she wasn't worth grieving over. Or we know that our sister's husband had been unfaithful and wonder why she is nonetheless sobbing over his death. What we think has nothing at all to do with the feelings of those who are in grief, and they will not be comforted by hearing us criticize their loved ones as not being deserving of their sorrow.

People who mourn the loss of their pets often comment on how little people understand about their grief. In the months that followed the death of my son, one of my dear friends experienced his own loss. His beloved dog died at the age of sixteen. When I reached out to him to express my condolences, he was taken aback by my concern. "Your loss is so much worse than mine," he said. I couldn't see his tears and think that his loss was any less painful or meaningful than mine. Every loss has meaning, and all losses are to be grieved—and witnessed. I have a rule on pet loss. "If the love is real, the grief is real." The grief that comes with loss is how we experience the depths of our love, and love takes many forms in this life.

Paul Denniston, my partner, teaches Grief Yoga. Sometimes he has people in his classes do an interaction that physicalizes witnessing. He has two people who are grieving stand facing each other and place their hands over their own hearts. They look into each other's eyes and say, "I witness your grief. I see your healing." This kind of witnessing of another's vulnerability can be very healing. Participants often say that they found it the most memorable, helpful moment in the session.

Unwitnessed Grief

Sometimes people can't bring themselves to be with a person who is grieving. Perhaps they fear they won't be able to find the right thing to say, or they think it will be too hard on them to show up. After my son David died, a friend kept calling me and leaving messages for weeks, until I finally picked up the phone. Maria told me how guilty she'd been feeling for not coming to the funeral. She knew David and me very well. "I just couldn't do it," she said. "I was afraid the pain would be too intense, and I didn't feel I could face you. But these days, I can't get you and David out of my mind and I feel a lot of guilt."

The fixer in me wanted to say, "Don't worry about it. It was no big deal," to ease her guilt. But that wasn't the truth. I just said, "I missed you."

Later I thought about what she had said, not only from a

grief perspective but from a life perspective. Something goes out of alignment when we try to avoid sadness and grief. If Maria had come to the funeral, she would have felt intense sadness and grief. But it would have been meaningful. It would have had an authenticity that came from moving with the rhythms of life. The sadness she felt would have gently melted her soul. Instead, she now had a river of guilt that ran through everything.

Life gives us pain. Our job is to experience it when it gets handed to us. Avoidance of loss has a cost. Having our pain seen and seeing the pain in others is a wonderful medicine for both body and soul.

In one of my lectures, a counselor said, "I have a client who can't go to funerals because she finds them too sad. What's the clinical term for that?"

I responded, "Selfish, self-centered." I wondered when people started to think they couldn't go to a funeral because it was going to be too sad. Life has peaks and valleys. It's our responsibility to be present for both.

In Maria's case, she failed to show up, which hurt me. Pain can also be caused by people who mean well but don't know how to be present. When you hear someone repeating his grief story over and over, that means his grief has not been witnessed in a healthy way. Perhaps one of his children said, "Dad, enough, we all know how Mom died. You have to stop dwelling on it." Or another child might have tried to comfort him by saying, "Don't be sad. Mom had a long life and at least she's not suffering anymore." Why doesn't he just move on? Repeating the story is often a griever's subconscious way of trying to get much-needed attention.

Another manifestation of not having grief witnessed is comparing one's loss to someone else's. "Can you believe Martha is complaining about the loss of her dog when my husband just died?" Comparing is a way of needing to be witnessed. It's saying, "Listen to me, not to Martha. My pain is worse. I need you to notice my pain."

The way to help is to make sure that the person who is grieving knows that she *does* have your attention, that you *are* listening, that she is welcome to talk to you about her feelings. "I see how much you are hurting," you can say, "and I know what a wonderful man your husband was. Do you remember the day we all went . . . " Some kind of opening like that might help her find a way to talk about her loss.

The Practical Griever

I met Lindy Chamberlain briefly in Australia long after her court trials were over and she was released from prison. I only had a moment to express my condolences for her loss. Based on the public's judgment of her grieving style, she could be the world's most well-known "practical griever." She gained international notoriety as Australia's embattled bereaved mother whose baby was taken by a dingo in 1980 while her family was camping. Meryl Streep authentically replicated her scream, "Dingo got my baby," in a movie about this horrible tragedy. Most believed she was guilty of the crime. Why? Because Lindy had a strong faith and did not publicly cry. She was found guilty of murder and received a life sentence with no parole. After many legal actions and DNA advancements, she was found not guilty. Finally in 2012, the public felt that Lindy had been fully exonerated.

Some grievers don't talk about their loss, they don't cry a river of tears. They get back to "normal" as soon as they can. Like Lindy, they appear too strong. Perhaps disconnected. Since they don't publicly or privately cry or share their feelings with friends and family, they are often misunderstood. We mistakenly think this relates to how much they loved the person. Nothing could be further from the truth. Such people may be labeled as having "delayed grief." It's assumed that one of these days, when the pressure of denying their feelings builds up, their grief will come flooding through. I've learned that some people are what I think of as "practical grievers." If you ask why they're not crying, they are likely to say something like, "I'd cry if it would bring them back, but it won't."

We must witness grief as it is. Practical grievers often complain that everyone is trying to change and fix them. They don't need to be fixed. They need to be seen and respected for their own way of dealing with loss.

Robert and Joan had been married for twenty-five years. One day, Robert answered the phone and learned that his brother, Corey, had died of a massive heart attack. He knew his parents and Corey's widow were too brokenhearted to take on the responsibility of planning everything, so he went right into "doing what needed to be done" mode. He was the point person for all the arrangements. His sister-in-law says to this day that she can't imagine how she could've gotten through this difficult period without Robert's help.

There were whispers at the funeral about how wonderfully Robert had stepped in, but had anyone seen him cry? No one had. Family members approached Joan privately and asked, "Has Robert cried with you?"

Joan had not seen him cry and she began to get worried. Over the next couple of weeks, she kept asking him how he was doing. "Do you miss Corey?"

"Of course I do," he said.

"I just want you to know it's okay to be sad."

"I know that and I am."

After about six weeks, Joan suggested that her husband go to a therapist. He was taken aback by the comment and asked her, "What's wrong? Is something going on?"

"Well, Corey died, and I'm worried you're not feeling it."

"I am feeling it. I don't cry like you, but I'm feeling it. I'm not sure what there is to say. He's gone. It's tragic. I'll miss him for the rest of my life. Nothing I say is going to bring him back."

Nine months later it was time for the annual fishing trip. Most of the men in the family got together each year for a weekend on a nearby lake. Joan was thrilled this was happening. She knew Robert's brother's absence would be deeply felt, since he had always been a part of the gathering. She was sure the men would talk about his death and this would give Robert a chance to process his feelings. When Robert returned, she said, "It must have been good for all of you guys to have a chance to talk to each other about Corey's death."

"We didn't mention it."

"How can that be?" Joan asked. "Corey was there last year and every year before, and he wasn't there this year. How could you not talk about it?"

She came to me because she felt Robert might be blocked. I suggested that although it was natural for her to grieve openly and expressively, he might be a practical griever, and he was probably dealing with his loss in the way that was natural to him. I asked her to imagine how she would feel if someone were to say to her, "Stop grieving," or, "You're grieving too much." Just as that would interfere with her natural way of processing loss, I explained, doing the opposite with Robert, telling him to show more emotion, was disrespectful to his way of grieving.

Joan realized she had to acknowledge Robert's way of grieving was as legitimate as crying a thousand tears.

From the Most Private to the Most Public

Simone was a talent booker for one of the late-night TV shows. One of the best in the business, she knew when a celebrity had a new film coming out or when there was a scandal in the making. It was her job to book the hottest stars at the peak of their fame.

Everyone knew Simone, but beyond the fact that she had a husband and grown children, few knew anything about her personal life. She rarely talked about it and was always careful to maintain a separation between her personal and her professional life.

One day Simone's assistant pulled her out of a meeting to take an urgent call. It was her daughter, saying that her husband had just died from a heart attack.

"What can I do to help?" her assistant asked. "What should I tell people?"

"Just tell them my husband died and I'll be back in two weeks. There's nothing more to say."

After two weeks, Simone returned to messages and flowers. She graciously accepted condolences, but when her fellow workers wanted details, she said she'd rather not talk about it. She had a "get back to work" attitude. But six months later, she turned in her resignation. Although her boss was sure she'd been snatched up by one of the rival networks, her resignation was much more complicated than that.

No one knew that Simone's husband had been bipolar. She'd spent years trying to keep him healthy, keep him on his meds, and help him be as productive as possible. Because of the stigma attached to her husband's illness, she had always been reluctant to talk about it, and her desire to protect his privacy had been reinforced by her own natural reserve. Work had been her escape from the difficulties of her home situation, a place where she didn't have to think about her husband's problems. But after his death, she found it hard to just keep going on.

When I met her, shortly after she'd left her job, she said she felt traumatized from the many years she'd spent taking care of and shielding him. She said that suddenly her work had begun to feel meaningless. She was reflecting on how few resources had been available to help her husband and she wanted to try to find a way to be more useful in the world. We talked about her going back to school and perhaps becoming a counselor or social worker. Neither of those resonated with her. However, she did have the resources to take some time off, and she decided she would use the time to think about her next moves.

I received a call from her about a year later, asking me to come and speak at the annual conference of an organization in a city far from where she had lived before.

"What's your involvement?" I asked her.

"Hang on a minute," she said. "I'm in my office and I need to close the door."

She explained to me that after her husband died, she knew she couldn't do anything about those twenty-five years of feeling helpless. But she wanted her next job to be something that would help her overcome that sense of wasted time. Eventually she found work at a national speaker's organization where instead of booking celebrities, she was booking some of the most important mental health care professionals in the country. "I wanted to do something to help people deal with their problems," she said. "I'm also volunteering at a mental health clinic."

"That's wonderful," I said. "Do your coworkers know why you made such a big life change?"

"David, you know me. I'm way too private for that. I just told them I wanted a change, so I moved out of LA."

That was Simone—private all the way. But being private hadn't meant she didn't feel her loss deeply. Nor did it get in the way of doing something meaningful to honor her husband.

At the other extreme, grief can be very public. One day my phone rang, and a woman's voice said, "I have Vice President Biden on the line." After a click, I heard his unmistakable voice saying, "Hey, David, this is Joe. I wanted to thank you for your writing."

Joe Biden was no newcomer to loss. Many years before, just as he was about to take office for his first term in the Senate, his wife, Neilia, and daughter, Naomi, were killed in a traffic accident. Two days after becoming a senator he had to deal with a mass shooting in New Orleans. Yes, the same one from my childhood. We spoke briefly about the strangeness of our lives and losses having intersected so closely back then, but what Vice President Biden wanted to talk about the day he called was a much more recent death—that of his son Beau, who had died of a brain tumor not long before.

I told him I thought the way he had handled his grief after

his son died was remarkable. He talked about his feelings openly and emotionally, at times even shedding tears in public, and he had described in an interview with Oprah Winfrey the intimate scene of him and his other son, Hunter, holding Beau's hand right before he died.

Just as it was Simone's style to keep her feelings to herself, it has always been Biden's style to let them out. But even though he had done so very movingly on several occasions after Beau died, his emotionalism was proving to be a challenge to him at that time. "As vice president," he said to me, "part of my job is to attend funerals and give eulogies, acting as an official representative of the government." He continued to do this even after the death of his son. Less than a month after Beau died he even found the strength to go to Charleston, South Carolina, to comfort the survivors of the horrific mass shooting at Emanuel African Methodist Episcopal Church. As he writes in his book *Promise Me, Dad: A Year of Hope, Hardship, and Purpose*, "The act of consoling had always made me feel a little better, and I was hungry to feel better." But he explained to me that day that since he himself was in deep grief, he was now finding that attending these funerals had become very challenging. They constantly returned him to his own feelings of loss.

I told him that I could imagine how hard this must be for him, but suggested that the death of his own son would make him especially sensitive to the pain of others. By mirroring their pain, he would be letting them know that their pain matters deeply, too. Moreover, this would be one way for him to find meaning from his son's death. I hope what I said was as helpful to him as something he has said many times to others in grief: "The time will come when memory will bring a smile to your lips before it brings a tear to your eyes." That's how it goes: pain first, meaning later.

Another person who was in the public eye when she lost someone she loved chose very consciously to make her loss visible to the entire world. When President Kennedy was shot in Dallas in 1963, his wife, Jacqueline Kennedy, refused to change the pink suit that was stained with his blood and his brains. "Let them see what they have done," she said. She didn't want the violence to be swept away. She wanted the horrific loss she was feeling to be fully witnessed. Having grief witnessed is about making loss real.

When Jackie Kennedy lost her husband, and Vice President Biden lost his son, they were both public figures. But for others, the tragedy of loss is what thrusts them into the public eye. This was the case for a young couple from Manhattan, Jayson and Stacy Greene, whom I met at one of my grief workshops at Kripalu, a retreat center in Stockbridge, Massachusetts. One morning their two-year-old daughter, Greta, was sitting on a bench on the Upper West Side of Manhattan with her grandmother when suddenly a piece of masonry fell eight stories, hitting Greta. The toddler was rushed to the hospital where she underwent emergency brain surgery, but she never regained consciousness and died.

Local media reported the tragedy and the story spread immediately, getting picked up by *The New York Times* and many other news outlets. *The Daily News* had used a photograph of Greta from her mother's Facebook page for a front-page story. Greta's parents quickly had become recognizable figures, and everywhere they went, well-meaning strangers would talk to them and offer condolences and ask questions. For Jayson and Stacy, in their fog of grief, these approaches felt intrusive. The attention was bewildering at a time when they were barely able to hold themselves together. They felt like the whole world was watching them grieve.

During the workshop, people were reading letters I had them write the night before. Jayson tentatively raised his hand in the back. When he read his letter to his daughter in a trembling voice, everyone in the room was shaken by their story. I knew they could feel it. I invited Jayson and Stacy to come to the front of the room and gave them permission to express all their negative feelings. I told them, "It's not uncommon for a couple whose child has died to be jealous of happy, carefree families.

It's normal in grief to feel anger. It's appropriate and inevitable. Anger even has its own stage in the grieving process. Let it out."

To encourage them, I took in the story and their pain as much as I could and began hitting the pillows I kept in the room for people to use to release their anger. Their pain was now in the room. I screamed for them, showing them that I was agonized and outraged that their daughter had died. They were shocked at my intensity in front of a room of people, but it ultimately gave them permission to have their own emotional outbursts. Jayson began drawing on an inner rage, and I started with him. I knew I was just a catalyst.

"I hate happy families!"

The room felt like it was with him as his hands hit the pillow. Stacy was behind him, watching Jayson with her hands in fists. But she had nowhere to go. Hardly realizing my own connection with her loss and anger, I turned to her like a coach in the last few moments of an important game and asked, "Stacy, what are you angry at?"

I could see her feeling anger and suppressing it at the same time.

"I don't know," she said.

"What kind of world do we live in," I said to the room and to God, "where your daughter's death would be allowed to happen?"

Jayson turned to me as a husband who was protective of his wife and her grief. He said, "Don't yell at her."

Stacy said, "The building was a center for seniors, and now when I walk around, I feel . . . When I walk past old people, I have a hard time." She took a deep breath. "They make me angry, so what am I supposed to do, walk around saying I hate old people?"

"Absolutely!" I said. "Everyone here knows what that means and that you don't really hate old people. You hate the time they have. You hate that they have lived full lives where Greta's was cut so short."

Stacy looked like she was unable to say it, especially with a few silver-haired people in the room. I looked around and said, "Let's all say, One . . . two . . . three: *I hate old people!*"

The people in the room were taking her anger very seriously, not personalizing it, but realizing that this was about the unfairness of time.

When we feel it, we release it and we can be free. It was a profound experience, not only for them. It affected everyone in the room who was there to witness their grief. I knew this would be the beginning of their healing.

Jayson called me months later and said, "I don't know if you remember me."

I told him I would never forget him or Greta and he was moved that I remembered. He told me that the weekend he spent in my workshop had been a tipping point. Until then, they had felt like they had been singled out for a tragedy. But being with so many others who had also experienced terrible losses had made them feel less victimized. This is part of what I think these grief workshops can accomplish—allowing those who are suffering to witness and reflect each other's pain.

Communal Mourning

Funerals and memorials are important. Something profound happens when others see and hear and acknowledge our grief. Mourning is the outward expression of our grief. Conversely, something goes wrong when it remains unseen. That's why I believe that when someone decides not to have a funeral, they're missing out. A funeral is the time for people to gather as a family, as a community, to witness grief together. The funeral is the most well-known ritual for death, a ceremony that creates meaning out of our loved one's experience of life, and our own experience of loss.

At a memorial, people talk about what the dead person meant to them. This may be in the form of a somber eulogy or a funny story. It can be accompanied by laughter or by tears—

or both. Whatever form it takes, telling the story of the loved one's life helps the mourners to accept the reality of death. It also helps us through the process of grieving. We need to hear the story from others, which helps us see things from a different perspective, and we need to tell it ourselves.

In the eulogy of Diana Spencer, Princess of Wales, her brother, Charles Spencer, told those who gathered in her honor, "Today is our chance to say thank you for the way you brightened our lives, even though God granted you but half a life. We will all feel cheated that you were taken from us so young, and yet we must learn to be grateful that you came along at all. Only now you are gone do we truly appreciate what we are now without and we want you to know that life without you is very, very difficult."

That is where the healing—and the meaning making—begins.

We think we can spare our children pain by not exposing them to the reality of death. But the opposite is true. Our children, just like us, are in pain when they lose someone they love, and it will not help them to have their pain glossed over. Going to a funeral will help because they, too, need to have their pain witnessed, to feel it reflected in the emotions of those around them.

When I explain funerals to young children, I'll say something like, "Do you remember last year when you went to Grandpa's house for his birthday gathering? Everyone sang 'Happy Birthday'? That's a way of saying I love you. Now that Grandpa has died, we're going to have a funeral for him and gather one last time in his honor to say goodbye. Saying goodbye is another way we say I love you."

The funeral ritual is important in witnessing grief because we will grieve alone for the rest of our lives. This is our last formal time to mourn together. One of the most common things we hear at funerals is that the deceased would not want us to grieve for them. I always think if we can't grieve at the funeral, when can we grieve? The funeral is by design a communal time to witness each other's grief through music, stories, poems, and prayers.

People often ask me, "Is a memorial better than a celebration of life?" My answer is one is not better than the other. They are both ways we witness our grief. In a memorial, we witness the sadness of the loss as well as honor their life. The celebration of life clearly moves the focus to celebrate what they meant to us when they were alive. I always remind people you can still cry at a celebration of life.

Ellen was a child of six who was very attached to her great-aunt, Ruth. They were inseparable, and when Ruth contracted brain cancer, she went to a nursing home to be cared for. Ellen missed her terribly and kept asking where her aunt was. Her mother said, "She's away resting."

Ellen kept asking when she would come back home, and her mother said, "Pretty soon."

A few weeks later, her mother told her that Ruth had died. Ellen climbed into her mother's lap and cried, but after a few minutes, her mother walked away, went upstairs to her bedroom, and shut the door. On the day of the funeral, Ellen's mother and father left the house to bury Ruth. Ellen begged to go along, but they said that the funeral was for grown-ups.

In my lectures I ask whether Ellen should have been allowed to go to the funeral. Both small and large groups always answer with a resounding yes!

I follow up with, "How many of you have issues or wounds because you were allowed to go to a funeral?" Occasionally I get a hand or two. Then I ask, "How many of you have issues, wounds, or trauma because you weren't allowed to go to the funeral?" About 15 percent of the hands in the room will go up.

We think skipping the pain helps our children, but the opposite is true. Our children, just like us, need their pain witnessed, and a funeral is important to them. When I was a child, sometimes our car would be slowed down because we were behind a hearse. We were used to seeing those black station wagons that picked up bodies at the hospital or someone's home. Now hearses are only used for the short drive between the service and the gravesite. Death has become sanitized, and the dead move around our cities in white unmarked vans. The next time you see a white van with no windows, you're probably behind a hearse.

People often tell me they are stuck in their loss. In the old days, there was just the funeral and the burial. People didn't have many choices. Now with cremation, there are many more options. We have the ability to personalize our final disposition as well as choose how and when we have a ceremony. That option to delay things is not just for cremation, but for the burial ceremony. These new choices also provide more opportunity for putting things off.

I often ask people questions about their loved one's memorial or celebration of life. More and more, the ones who are stuck in grief say, "We didn't have one. It just wasn't practical." Or "Everyone was busy. We were thinking of doing one in six months when everyone could plan," or "but now too much time has passed," or "now another family member has died."

When someone is struggling with their grief, and I ask about the final remains, they often tell me the ashes are temporarily in the closet until they figure out what to do with them.

Ceremonies commemorating a loss are not supposed to be practical, easy, or come at a perfect time. When our loved ones die, it is the moment when grief is most palpable and witnessing is most needed. There is no completion of grief or closure, but that last ceremony is a bookend that acknowledges that the final chapter of life has ended. There seems to be an ever-growing inconclusiveness when the life of a loved one is not marked by an event.

We need a sense of community when we are in mourning because we were not meant to be islands of grief. The reality is that we heal as a tribe. There is no greater gift you can give someone in grief than to ask them about their loved one, and then truly listen. When we see our sorrow in the eyes of another, we know our grief has meaning. We get a glimpse, maybe for the first time since the loss, that we will survive, and a future is possible.

CHAPTER THREE

The Meaning of Death

Without suffering and death, human life cannot be complete.

—Viktor Frankl

We can't talk about grief without talking about its predecessor, death. Why discuss death in a book about grief? Because *the death shapes the grief*. If our loved one had what we believe to be a meaningful death, our grief is likely to be less tormented. If we are mourning a more problematic death, we are likely to have a more complicated grief. Through our efforts during the dying process, we can help bring more meaning to it for both ourselves and the dying person. Of course, some deaths are inevitably going to be more complicated than others, such as a death by suicide, an overdose, the death of a child, a sudden death, the death of someone we loved but were estranged from, to name just a few.

What we often do in my grief work classes and workshops is to go back and revisit the death and the days leading up to it. Did the person have to die? Could the death have been prevented? Could I have prevented it? Could someone else have? How did the dying person experience what was happening? Was there something I should have done to make it easier? Where is the meaning in death and dying?

Annie's best friend, Betty, became ill with cancer when she was in her forties. Betty had a loving husband and two kids. They were determined to fight the cancer aggressively and she

spent the next few years undergoing chemo and radiation procedures to slow the progression of the cancer. Betty and her
husband felt like these challenges deepened their relationship
and enhanced their appreciation for each other and their family. There were moments that would suddenly seem so special
to Betty that she would kneel and kiss her kids and tell them
how grateful she was to have them in her life.

But Betty's friend Annie couldn't see any of the good that
Betty found in her experience. She would go on and on about
what a tragedy her illness was, how unfair. "This is just so terrible," she'd say to Betty. "Your life is filled with doctors and
chemo and cancer groups."

Betty said, "Yes, but I get to meet a lot of wonderful people
in those cancer groups. And I treasure the time I spend with my
husband and my kids in a way I might not have done if I wasn't
aware that my days may be short."

"But you're just so sick all the time," Annie said.

Betty took her hand. "But I'm also so loved all the time."

This is an example of two people bringing different meaning to the same story. It wasn't that Betty found the chemo
or the disease enjoyable. She said that when the pain came, it
was all-consuming, and the idea of dying and leaving her husband and children was terrible. But Betty found the time with
her loved ones deeply meaningful. She also enjoyed the new
relationships she was making in her support groups. She said,
"These are some of the most courageous people I've ever met."

Annie could only see the injustice of her best friend being ill.
Her worldview held that bad things shouldn't happen to good
people, and she could find no other way of looking at the story
of what was happening to Betty. How she was raised and her
own experience of loss probably shaped her view of life and
illness.

Meaning Making through Stories

I often teach that in grief, *pain is inevitable, but suffering is optional*. In my lectures, I make that distinction because most of us think of them as interchangeable. They are not. Pain is the pure emotion we feel when someone we love dies. The pain is part of the love. Suffering is the noise our mind makes around that loss, the false stories it tells because it can't conceive of death as random. Death can't just happen. There must be a reason, a fault. The mind looks for where to lay the blame, perhaps on ourselves, perhaps on someone else. Our loved one died not because of the cancer, but because the nurse gave morphine for pain management. Or their life ended because we put them in hospice, not because they were dying with an end-stage disease.

We blame another for the death of our loved one rather than the terminal illness she'd been sick with for two years. Our own version of our loved one's death—the story we tell ourselves about it—can either help us heal or keep us mired in suffering.

In a way, meaning both *begins* and *ends* with the stories we tell. Storytelling is a primal human need. The meaning begins with our own version of the story of our loved one's death. We all have a stock of stories that explain who we are, what we think, what we dream about, what we fear, what family has meant to us, and what we've accomplished.

Having those stories to tell is part of being human. We tell them all the time to family, friends, and strangers. But we also tell stories to ourselves, and when we do, the way we frame them has the power to change our feelings. In my grief workshops and retreats I often ask people to write about their loved ones' deaths. This practice has been inspired in part by the work of social psychologist James Pennebaker of the University of Texas. He knew that people who experienced a traumatic event were more depressed, emotionally volatile, and died of cancer and heart disease at higher rates than those who had not experienced a traumatic event, which didn't surprise him. What did surprise him was that people who kept their trauma a secret experienced significantly higher rates of death than those who had spoken about it. This made him wonder whether sharing secrets would improve their health. It turned out that they didn't even have to share their secrets with others to benefit. Simply writing them down had a positive effect. His research showed that they went to the doctor less often, lowered their blood pressure, and had better (lower) heart rates. They also had fewer feelings of anxiety and depression.

The writing proved to be healing in three areas:

1. Examining causes and consequences: They used more words and phrases like *understand, realize, because,* and *work through.*
2. Shift in perspective: They went through a change in pronouns from *I* and *me* to *he* and *she*. They looked outside their own heads and into the minds of others.
3. Finding positive meaning in the traumatic experience: The meaning does not negate the "bad" but they found that some good can come out of even the worst events.

I can testify from my personal experience how helpful this can be. As I've often recounted at my workshops and lectures, I've used storytelling to guide me through the grief work I've done over the death of my mother. The pain I felt from her death lasted many years because there was so much unresolved anger and hurt complicating my grief. I told the story of that death many times over, which simply reinforced my longstanding feelings of victimhood. But eventually I decided to write about it instead in the voices of the other two people most central to the story: my parents.

First I wrote about it in the voice of my father. I had always judged him harshly for how poorly he handled my grief. Late one night, not long after my mother died, I got out of bed and went into his room. "Dad," I asked, "do you think Mom still exists and she could still be around us?"

"It's late," he said. "Go back to bed."

I didn't know what to make of that response. Maybe he just wasn't grieving like I was. Maybe he hadn't loved her. Or maybe I was asking the wrong questions. I couldn't understand why we weren't talking about my mother. But we never did, so I was left to grieve in isolation. I realize now that my father was not a man who trafficked in the world of feelings. I never heard him talk about his grief or anyone else's. He was a problem solver who was always trying to figure out how to do the next thing. Grief, however, was not something he saw as a problem that might deserve attention.

Years later, when I decided to write his side of the story, I imagined for the first time what it must have been like for him to lose his wife and become a single parent caring for a thirteen-year-old child. My mom had always been the hands-on parent. He was the provider. Now he had a whole new role to play on top of everything else he was dealing with. I could see what an overwhelming situation this must have been for him. I thought of him overworked, in deep grief at the end of a long day, and then being awakened from sleep by his son asking him strange hypothetical questions that he had no idea how to answer. Instead of judgment, I found compassion for him.

Then I wrote the story from my mother's point of view. She had spent so much of her life in and out of hospitals, frequently in intensive care units. I wasn't told much about what was happening, and my only recollection of those hospital stays was that she occasionally left for a few days. From my viewpoint, it was like having my mom go on a business trip. Now I can only imagine what that must have entailed. I never thought about how frightening that must have been for her.

When she did come home, I never asked her about where she'd been and she never said. What could it have been like for her to know she was dying and leaving behind her husband and her son? I realized how painful it must have been for her. The shift in the story also enabled me to understand for the first time that my mother hadn't abandoned me. My mother had died, but abandonment was how my young mind had interpreted it. The story I'd been telling myself about my mother's death had been my prison for years. When I retold it through the eyes of my parents and realized how hard her sickness and death must have been for them, and how much they loved me and tried to protect me from being hurt, it became my freedom. I felt a deep gratitude to them.

The words we use to describe our experiences are powerful things. Jayson, the man who came to my workshop with his wife, Stacy, after the death of their daughter, Greta, later wrote a book, *Once More We Saw Stars*, about their loss and their subsequent journey toward healing. When he called me to tell me about the book, he also told me that Stacy had become pregnant shortly after the workshop and had just given birth to a son. I said that I thought that writing a book and having a baby both sounded like wonderful ways of finding meaning in the wake of tragedy. He agreed.

As he explained to an interviewer, "I'm a person of words. They're the way I process everything. Writing is a way not to be blinded by grief, and to maintain a connection with Greta . . . I honestly believe it kept me alive."

He believed that the meaning he was able to find through writing had helped him to move forward. "Greta is gone," he said, "but she's still with us. I want the book to be life-affirming and hopeful, because I'm alive to write it. I think that's important."

Jayson's book will be his way of honoring his daughter and giving an example to his son. It will also offer comfort to others who have lost loved ones, letting them know that they are not alone in their grief, that they, too, will be able to make sense of their suffering.

Death Be Not Proud

"Death be not proud" is the first line of a seventeenth-century sonnet by John Donne, which has been used to comfort mourners for centuries with the idea that death is only a portal to eternal life. This is one way of not allowing death to be seen as some kind of triumph over us. But we do not have to believe in an afterlife to reframe our idea of death, to see it as a portal to meaning.

One of the most important lessons I learned in writing my first book, *The Needs of the Dying*, is that the way we view death reflects how we look at life. If death is simply an enemy that triumphs over us in the end, a horrible trick of nature that defeats us, then our lives are meaningless. Too often the language we use about death reinforces that idea. In our modern society, death is spoken of as a failure, as though it were optional, and if only we fought hard enough against it we could defeat it—despite the fact that our mortality rate is 100 percent. A physician cannot write "old age" as a cause of death on a death certificate. There must be a reason, and unfortunately that reason turns out to be some kind of "failure." For the hundred-year-old man who had a wonderful long life that he lived to the fullest until he went to sleep one night and didn't wake up, it must be listed as "cardiac *failure*" or "respiratory *failure*."

Illness, too, is a "failure." All too often in the medical world, you're not Mrs. Hanson, the woman who lost her husband in a car accident, then went to college at night and opened her own business, all while raising three children and sending them to college. Instead, you're "the kidney failure" or "the heart failure in room 302."

That sense—and language—of failure permeates everything in our final chapter of life. Listen to how we speak about death and write about it in obituaries: *She succumbed to the illness. He lost the battle to cancer.* Or *Dad didn't make it.*

Apparently, no matter how great our life, we are destined to fail in the end. That doesn't have to be our understanding of either life or death, however.

Actress Edie Falco, known for her roles on *The Sopranos* and *Nurse Jackie*, was interviewed about her experience with breast cancer. The interviewer said, "So you're a winner! You beat cancer."

She said, "No, I was very lucky. I had a treatable cancer. Not everyone has a treatable cancer, and I don't want to make myself a winner, because that would mean there are losers, and we are all in this battle."

I thought about her insight into life's endgame of winners and losers. I have a cancer support group and lecture called "Bogeyman in the Closet" that I do at UCLA and the Cancer Support Community where we deal with the fear of recurrence, which is actually the fear of death. I called it this because of how parents handle children's fear of the bogeyman. They turn on the lights, open the closet door, and show them there is nothing to fear. The fear is in their minds. That's what I do with my cancer groups. I remind them that fear doesn't stop death. Fear does stop life, however, but it doesn't have to. If we allow ourselves to live with the consciousness of death, it will enrich us by making us understand how precious life is. Confronting the reality that we are born, we flourish, and when our time comes, we die, we will live our lives from a meaningful place and live our deaths in a meaningful way.

Often, families who receive bad news from the doctor about a loved one's terminal illness plead, "You can't let them die. They can't die." We have seen that if instead they asked, "What can we do to help him make the most of the time he has left?" they would be asking a question that would lead to a better end of life for their loved one and a better experience of grief for them.

We want to ignore death, forget it, deny it. But it will come to all of us. It's the change that happens whether we want it to or not. If met head-on, the prospect of death, its inevitability, can bring new meaning to life.

In the production I saw of Thornton Wilder's play *Our Town*, Emily, played by Helen Hunt, dies in childbirth but is allowed to return to her life for just one day. She wants it to be a milestone day of some sort, maybe her wedding day, but one of the other dead counsels her to choose "the least important day in your life. It will be important enough." She chooses her twelfth birthday, an ordinary day in her completely ordinary small town with her totally ordinary family—except that when she returns to it from the dead, she realizes that all of it was extraordinary. Overwhelmed by how beautiful even the most unremarkable of days on earth is, she says, "It goes so fast. We don't have time to look at one another . . . I didn't realize. So, all that was going on and we never noticed."

Her awareness of what she lost is so excruciating that she chooses to go back to the grave even before the end of the day she has been granted. Before she leaves, she takes one last look: "Goodbye, goodbye, world. Goodbye, Grover's Corners . . . Mama and Papa . . . and Mama's sunflowers. And food and coffee. And new-ironed dresses and hot baths . . . and sleeping and waking up. Oh, earth, you're too wonderful for anybody to realize you." She turns then to the Stage Manager and asks him if anybody ever does realize it while they're still alive. And he says, "No . . . the saints and poets, maybe . . . "

Wilder could well have had Dylan Thomas's poem "Do Not Go Gentle into That Good Night" in mind when he invoked the wisdom of poets (though in fact *Our Town* was written a decade before Thomas's poem). When Thomas commanded us to "Rage, rage against the dying of the light" in his poem, we hear in it a howl of grief at the knowledge that all lives must end. But we can also hear an invitation to witness and celebrate the "light" of every day that dawns for us.

The saints and poets may know how to see the gift of our days, but most of us do not. We are devastated when our days

with someone we love comes to an end. We don't appreciate those days until it's too late. But painful as it is, if we can
view the approach of death as a reminder to us to value every
moment, we can find new sources of meaning.

Death Makes Life Valuable

When Jennifer, a former coworker of mine, received what she
thought was a death sentence, she made it into an invitation to
life. She told me:

> In 1985, I was twenty-nine years old and I'd just gone through
> a divorce when I was diagnosed with Hodgkin's lymphoma. I
> thought, "I can't see what's going on in me, but whatever it is,
> it can't take away who I really am; my essence, my spirit, and
> my soul." I never asked, "Why me?" Instead, I said, "Okay,
> what do we do now?" I underwent the recommended treat-
> ments and got through them okay. I realized that we don't
> always have tomorrow.
>
> I'm not the most self-motivated person unless it's some-
> thing I really, really want to be doing, so I tend not to make
> big changes. I always wanted to go to graduate school, but I
> never did. Now I was sick. I thought, "I'm going to die. If not
> now, someday. This life is a *limited-time offer* and the ride
> will end at some point." Death has a way of creating urgency.
> I knew death was at the end of the ride.
>
> I looked at my life and wondered, "Have I really done all I
> can?" I pictured a roller coaster of life with its ups and downs.
> I was looking down at life. Meaning for me was about taking
> the whole ride.
>
> I began to imagine what was on the next ride. I started look-
> ing up catalogs in the library and applied to graduate school.
> I was still getting treatments when I was accepted and wasn't
> feeling at all well, but it would be months until I started the

course. I figured if I had to bow out at the last moment, dying would be an acceptable excuse. But I didn't die.

I started school and got my master's in social work. A major part of the meaning I've found is that because of my training and personal experience, I know how to be present for people who are going through difficult situations. I don't pretend I have all the answers, but since I know what it's like for them, I do have deeper empathy and I know how to inspire hope. I'll tell someone who looks hopeless at the cancer institute where I work that I am a cancer survivor. Usually the person will say something like, "So you beat it!" I say, "No. I've surrendered to death and to life. To the whole ride."

Jennifer understood that although she had no control over what would happen tomorrow with her illness, there was one thing she could control: how she would respond. That was how she found meaning and how Viktor Frankl says we all can.

The urgency created by the prospect of death was also a factor in the way Farrah Fawcett responded to her illness. Most people remember the actress as an icon, the larger-than-life pinup girl on a bathing suit poster. Others loved her as Jill Munroe on *Charlie's Angels*. *TV Guide* ranked her as one of the fifty greatest TV stars of all time. She went on to prove her talent as a serious actress in the movie and stage versions of *Extremities* and in the film *The Burning Bed*, and she played many other roles, too. But one role she never expected to play was that of an activist in the fight against cancer.

Instead of asking "Why me?" when she was diagnosed, she made it clear that she did not intend to be a victim. Not only would she fight cancer, she would make a documentary about that fight to inspire others and fund a foundation that would help them with their own struggles. Alana Stewart, her best friend, helped film her medical journey. In the documentary, Fawcett says, "In a way, I'm almost glad I got cancer. Now I know I can make a difference." Later she asks: "Why is there not more research into certain types of cancer? Why doesn't our health system embrace alternative treatments that have proved successful in other countries?" She hoped her foundation would help answer those questions and others.

Fawcett finishes the documentary by responding to another question: "How *are* you?" Her answer: "Today I've got cancer, but on the other hand, I'm alive! So . . . right now, I'm great. My life goes on and so does my fight. And, by the way, how are you? What are you fighting for?"

The actress's life did not continue, but the good she did lives on. Fawcett was very clear that after her death she did not want her likeness exploited, but rather used for good, for something meaningful. So she left her fortune as well as her likeness—which was perhaps her greatest asset, and one that continues to generate revenues—to her foundation. Ten years after she died, the foundation is still providing funds for cutting-edge research, treatment, and prevention of cancer.

I never met Farrah. Her meaning making was our introduction. Today I volunteer as a board member on the Farrah Fawcett Foundation, helping to decide how her gifts—her money and her likeness—can be best used in the fight against cancer. While she was dying, she searched for meaning, found it, and implemented it. In death, the meaning she found has become her legacy, and I find meaning in helping to make her dream of aiding others with cancer a reality.

What's Meaningful?

Foundations and movies are wonderful legacies to leave behind. But meaning can seep into our lives through moments as simple as eating an ice cream sundae. Lois shared with me the following story:

My mantra is "What's meaningful?" I ask it all the time. It guides me. I'm a nurse practitioner and I work with kidney and liver transplant patients. I was introduced to meaning and death through my parents. I always contacted them the night before I went on a trip. One night when I had finished talking with my mom, I asked her if my dad was around. His seventieth birthday was the next day and I wanted to wish him an early happy birthday.

"He just lay down," she said.

"That's okay," I said. "I'll call tomorrow from California." I still regret that moment. I should have told my mom to bring the phone to him. As soon as I got off the plane, I had a call from my brother telling me that my dad had passed away. He was a healthy active man we expected to live for many more years, but he never got back up after he lay down. Speaking to him would have given me such a meaningful memory. Instead I missed my last opportunity to have that connection. That's why I always ask now, "What would be the most meaningful?"

I try never to lose an opportunity to tell someone that I love them and what they mean to me. Three years later, my mom was diagnosed with cancer, and since the cancer was advanced and untreatable, the doctors felt that she would be better served with pain management than with any attempt to prolong her life. I moved her in with me. I knew that would be meaningful for both of us. She received palliative care and then hospice care at my home. Her bed was in my living room and she was able to look out at the garden and play with my dogs.

Then on top of everything, I got appendicitis and had an appendectomy. I was going to have to use up all my paid time off for my illness. So many worries and concerns were swirling through my head until I remembered to ask myself what would be meaningful in that situation. This is a gift, I realized, because I will have two weeks off work, every minute of which my mother and I can spend together. It's not anything that anyone can take away from us. We ate ice cream sundaes for dinner every night, and during the days we got to talk about things we might never otherwise have shared. It was awesome. A lot of people told me they couldn't believe how bad my timing was. I said, "Actually, no, it worked out pretty well. I got to be home with Mom."

About six weeks later, Mom's health was declining. One Sunday night, she called out at nine thirty, "I need to see your brothers. Now."

"Okay," I said, wondering what this was all about. Maybe she knew something I didn't. So I called my brothers to come over, even though it was so late. One of them said, "Are you kidding me?"

With my past experience of missing my last chance to speak to my father, I wasn't going to take no for an answer. "She's saying she wants to see you. I don't think you should ignore this. You have to do what she wants," I told him.

Everyone came over. There were eight or nine of us gathered when my mom said to me, "Do we have any chips and dip?"

It was ten o'clock on a Sunday night and I thought, "She really wants chips and dip? Okay," I decided, "chips and dip it is." We all sat around eating chips and dip. She passed away about five days later. It was the last time we were all together before she died.

I love what Lois did. Simply asking what's meaningful can change our experience of imminent death. It can change lives as it changed Lois's. But for so many, the last chapter of life is not the most interesting one, nor the most important. We almost see it as a meaningless, "throwaway" part of life. Instead of using the precious time to complete relationships, to express our love, we allow the final chapter to become a series of medical issues to be conquered, a frantic search for a cure when one is no longer possible. We don't know how to watch our loved ones go peacefully into the sunset. We need to ask ourselves what we can do to make the last chapter of life meaningful.

Fran grew up with a very stoic mother. She was never one

to be affectionate. As an adult, Fran said to her mother, "I love you, Mom. We never say it out loud and I want you to know I love you." Her mother looked at her, puzzled. Fran said, "Don't you want to say it back?"

"Oh, honey, that's ridiculous. We're mother and daughter. Of course we love each other."

Years later, when Fran's mother was ninety-six, she was dying in Fran's home with hospice nurses in attendance. One night Fran was at her mother's bedside as she was drifting in and out of consciousness. The hospice nurse turned to Fran and said, "I bet she'd like it if you massaged her hands and feet."

Fran said, "Oh, you don't know my mother. I could never even hug her."

The nurse said, "People change at the end of their lives. We all need a little extra tenderness at the beginning of our lives and at the end."

Fran paused and took that in. She gently reached for her mother's hand and began caressing it. Surprisingly, a sweet smile that she hadn't seen in years appeared on her mother's face. She turned to the nurse as she continued to gently rub her mother's hand, "Oh my gosh! She never let me do anything like this before. It feels so good to be able to touch her."

After her mother died, Fran said that the time she had spent massaging her was the most meaningful time they'd had together in years. Sometimes we can find unexpected meaning in the smallest of things.

There are times we cannot be with our loved ones. Brenda was raising her three-year-old daughter, Jenny, with the help of friends and neighbors while her husband was deployed in Iraq. As a consultant she could work at home.

Brenda needed to go into the city for a few hours to meet with a client. Jenny was left with her neighbor, who often babysat. The neighbor was raking while Jenny played ball a few feet away. A car going by lost control when its driver had a seizure and drove right into the front yard, hitting Jenny and knocking her into the street. A nearby police officer drove up immediately and stopped his car in the middle of the street to shield the girl from any other traffic. After calling for an ambulance he picked up the little girl and held her in his arms. The paramedics arrived just as she stopped breathing. They took the girl and began life support.

The hospital frantically tried to reach her mother to let her know her daughter was in a horrific accident. After Brenda's presentation, she checked in with her neighbor and heard what happened and drove to the hospital. When she arrived she learned the doctors were not able to save Jenny's life. Four hours after the accident occurred the nurses, social workers, and chaplains sat in the small room consoling her and letting her know that everything that could be done had been done.

Family members and friends were beginning to gather and they needed to move the devastated mother to a larger room. As she walked through the emergency room, the police officer who'd been first on the scene approached her and said, "I just want you to know your daughter was not alone."

In the months that followed, Brenda and her husband's only meaning was knowing that her daughter was cared for in her final moments. Even if that person was a stranger.

The Love That Lives On

Everything that lives must die. But while life has to end, love doesn't. As the sun sets on the final days of someone we love, we may indeed want to "rage against the dying of the light." But it's worth reflecting on the fact that although we perceive the sun as setting, that's only because the earth is rotating, turning away from the sun. Soon it will turn back, and we will begin a journey toward another day. Is that also true for our loved ones?

How you answer that may depend on your religious and/or spiritual views. If you believe in an afterlife, then you will believe that your loved one will indeed live on. But even if you have no such belief in which to find comfort, the end of your loved one's life is not the end of your relationship, since your love lives on. Just as my relationship with my mother has continued to evolve in the half century since she died, all of us have the potential not just to hold on to the love we had, but to nourish and grow it.

When I work with the family of someone who's dying, I often take family members aside and ask, "Do you ever go into the room while your loved one is sleeping?"

They typically reply, "Of course."

I ask them what they do when they're in the room, and they always have the same answer, "I just sit there staring at him."

"The next time you're with him and he falls asleep," I suggest, "take your chair and turn your back to him."

I explain to them that we have an emotional and physical relationship with our loved ones as well as a spiritual relationship. In our day-to-day lives, we rely on the physical. We know our loved ones are here because we can see and touch and hear them. But just as the person who loses one of his senses finds that the other senses become stronger—such as when a person goes blind and suddenly begins to hear much more acutely—we have the capacity to create a stronger emotional and spiritual relationship when the physical relationship is coming to an end. I suggest that when they're sitting in the chair facing away from the bed, unable to rely on sight, they should try to sense the fullness of their loved one's presence through these other modes of perception.

Death is the ultimate change, the ultimate end. It is a change we think we can't understand and an ending we think we can't survive. But although the change happens whether we want it to or not, we can find freedom in accepting it, and in understanding it as a prelude to something else.

When people go to a hospice or a nursing home, many of them don't know why there are butterflies painted on the walls. Shortly after the end of World War II, when Elisabeth Kübler-Ross visited different concentration camps, she saw pictures of butterflies etched into the walls everywhere she looked. She found it very strange that people who were dying would draw butterflies. She said it wasn't until many years later, when she began working with dying children and noticed that they, too, would draw butterflies, that she finally understood why. She realized that for the dying butterflies were a symbol of transformation, not of death, but of life continuing, no matter what. Although your relationship with your loved one will change after death, it will also continue, no matter what. The challenge will be to make it a meaningful one.

CHAPTER FOUR

The First Step in Finding Meaning

In the depths of winter, I finally learned that within me lay an invincible summer.

—Albert Camus

The first step in finding meaning is the fifth stage of grief: acceptance. We don't like loss. We will never be okay with it, but we must accept it, even in its brutality and, in time, acknowledge the reality of it.

Acceptance doesn't happen all at once. You accept *some* of the reality that your loved one is gone when you make arrangements at the funeral home. But the acceptance is only partial. The death still isn't real to you. You'll be cycling back and forth between the various stages of grief for some time to come, perhaps spending long months in one stage, only brief days in another. Acceptance grows slowly in us.

In the first months after my son's death, I stood over his grave and yelled, "Is this going to be the rest of my life, standing over your grave?" I turned to the skies in search of God and asked, "How could you let an accident like this happen?" I was traumatized, grief-stricken, and in a rage.

In my mind I fast-forwarded to images of years to come, picturing myself stuck forever in that moment, my son David still missing, my pain never-ending. I kept my gaze on the heavens, walking back and forth as I said, "Really, David? Really, God? This is going to be it?"

That is what acceptance looked like for me early on. I visited David's grave and I accepted that he was dead. My limited acceptance was only because I saw his body go into the ground. Otherwise, I couldn't believe he was gone. But that early acceptance was also mixed with anger, and in my anger I thought my pain would always be that enormous.

Three years later, the scene looked very different. I lay quietly at David's grave, looking down at the grass and up to the heavens and saying, "This is it, David. This is our life." For me, it was a moment of deep acceptance. With a lot of help and support, I'd moved beyond anger and found some peace.

To find that peace, we cannot skip over the challenging stages of acceptance. It's not unusual for me to see people early on in their grief trying to jump into meaning prematurely. They feel a temporary rush of purpose. Perhaps they're speaking out about a cause that was important to their loved one, or they're starting a foundation. Or raising awareness about the circumstances of their loved one's death. I often see these people a year later, after they have given the speeches or started their foundations, when they find themselves newly overwhelmed with grief. Often they will sound like I did early on at David's grave. "So this is going to be my life now? Giving speeches and running a foundation? That's it?"

They have to recalibrate their grief. I tell them, "I'm so glad you were able to move forward so fast and find so much meaning, but you might need to go back and revisit some of the earlier stages, like anger or acceptance or both."

For most of us, the first step in making meaning out of loss is fully experiencing all the stages of grief, which means feeling the depths of pain and taking the time to live there for a while. When we have lived in that painful reality, we can begin to find a more peaceful place of acceptance and meaning can start to firmly put down its roots. In other situations we are slowly finding the acceptance, but having a hard time leaving those painful moments.

In my workshops I ask people to write down what parts of their loved ones' deaths they have accepted and what parts they haven't. This exercise guides them to the areas of their grief that have not yet been resolved. It leads them to the feelings that still need to be expressed. That is where their work and healing lie—in those feelings.

I love the quote, "If I had my life to live over again, I would find you sooner so that I could love you longer." Whoever wrote it wrote from a place of acceptance, an understanding of the inevitability of death.

I was sitting with a grieving woman who was telling me how painful her life was without her husband. I listened patiently and recognized the pain she was feeling in the moment, but I was listening for something else. She looked at me in tears and said, "This pain will never end." When I hear this from a person in grief, I understand why she is suffering so deeply.

"Your pain will not always be like this," I told her. "It will change." This is a message that the grieving need to hear, and in the moment of saying it, I often observe a shift. The person looks up at me and says, "It will?" And he or she suddenly becomes lighter.

When I do this with someone in front of an audience, they are shocked at the visible change they witness. They want to know what I did that brought about the shift. It all goes back to letting the person know that while pain from loss is inevitable, suffering is optional. I tell the person, "I cannot take away your pain. It's not my place to do that. Your pain is yours. It's part of the love you feel. What I can do, however, is to let you know that if you look for meaning, your pain will change, your suffering will end."

When the voice in someone's mind is whispering that they will always feel what they are feeling, now I can interrupt that voice by offering the possibility of a way out, a future—through meaning.

The mind can be cruel in grief. Concentration camp survivors often talk about the horrific situations they had to endure. The physical suffering was unbearable. But they also talk about the internal suffering they experienced when they were unable to picture a future. The torture of not knowing when they would get out, if ever, was even worse than their other tortures. The thought of a future without a release date deprived them of any sense of purpose and condemned them to the horrors of the present. But as long as you are alive you have a future, and the promise of release from your current pain.

To bring this idea to life, on the first day of retreats, I often ask people to write a letter to their past. They usually write something about how wonderful life was when their loved ones were still alive and how terrible it is without them. They write about past losses, the horrible wounds of yesterday, and all their losses.

On the second day, I ask them to write letters to their future selves. They write sympathy letters, such as, I'm sorry you still hurt so much. Then we talk about the fact that their future lives may be very different from what they have imagined. Hard as it is to understand this now, the future doesn't have to be—and probably won't be—the way they think it will be.

On the last day, I ask them to write another letter about the future they envision for themselves. I ask them to write in all caps on the top, MY FUTURE. Then I sit. They wait awkwardly for further instructions. I remain quiet until someone eventually asks, "Are you going to tell us what to write or give us some direction?"

"Sure," I respond. "Look at your paper. What do you see?"

Someone shouts out, "A blank piece of paper."

"Yes. *That* is your future," I say. "Blank. It isn't written yet. You are the writer. Not your past, not your losses, not death. But you. You are the creator of your future. Don't let your mind tell you otherwise. Your future is blank as of now. As the saying goes, *Don't let your past dictate your future.*"

The Meaning of Our Thoughts

How do our minds create the future? What role do your thoughts play in all of this? After loss, do you have any control over anything, much less your mind? Can you do anything to shape the meaning you attach to what has happened?

The answer is yes, you do have control. Your thoughts create meaning. Meaning guides the story in your mind, the story you tell yourself as well as the story you tell others. I'm healing versus I'm stuck. I will never live again versus I will live a life to honor my loved one.

I was in New York a few months after David died and saw a friend. I ran into him again last year after I had broken my arm in Australia. During that second visit, he said, "You are always wounded, first emotionally, now physically."

I said, "No, I'm always healing when I see you."

The story you tell yourself repeatedly becomes your meaning. Just as the story I told myself for many years about the past—about my mother's death—kept me imprisoned in pain, the story I began to tell myself from other points of view freed me. So, too, can the stories you tell yourself about the future help to free you from the pain you are feeling now.

When you notice your interpretation of a story, notice your tone and your perception of the past and future. Think about the meaning you are bringing to it:

Original Meaning	*New Meaning*
This death happened to me.	Death happens.
I'm a victim.	I am a victor because I have survived this loss.
This death was a punishment.	Death is usually random.

Original Meaning	*New Meaning*
Why did this happen to me?	Everyone gets something this lifetime.
It happened because of something.	There was nothing I could have done.
My story is the saddest one.	My story had very sad parts.

Along with having people examine the way they perceive and tell their stories, I ask them to remove two words from their vocabulary: *never* and *always*. When someone says they'll never be happy again, I tell them it may be true, but research shows it doesn't have to be true. They will often respond with, "Not after this horrible event has happened to me." I tell them about a study years ago in *The Journal of Personality and Social Psychology* that compared lottery winners to people who were paralyzed in accidents. It seemed to show that we have an internal baseline for happiness. In the long term, winning the lottery didn't increase happiness as much as others thought it would, and a catastrophic accident didn't make people as unhappy as one might expect. Your life will never be the same, but happiness again is still possible. Never being happy again is a statement about the future. But no one can predict the future. All they can know for sure is that they are unhappy today. It helps to say, "I'm unhappy today," and leave it at that.

In one of my grief groups, I was working with someone whose son had died unexpectedly a few years earlier. She told me that she was deeply saddened by the image of her son in the morgue. Since we were dealing with grief and not trauma, I told her it might be possible to change her thoughts since they were reminding her of one horrible moment.

"I can't do that," she said.

"But we have to question that concept in grief," I said. "Can you really not change your thoughts? Every day we choose our thoughts. As a society, we don't have much awareness of that.

We have to unlearn the belief that we have no power over what happens in our minds."

She interrupted me, "David, the images just come at me and make me so sad."

"I'm sure they do. That breaks my heart. But let's try something. Could you all just take a moment and close your eyes? I'd like you to picture a big purple elephant. Raise your hand when you have that image."

Within a second, all hands went up. They opened their eyes and I told them, "I just changed your thoughts. I made 100 percent of the people in this room think of a purple elephant. We *do* have power to change our thoughts." Even in its simplicity this exercise reminds them they do have control. Imagine the thoughts in your mind as being like a garden. Whatever thoughts you water are the thoughts that will grow. When you have a horrible image in your mind, if you keep looking at it and telling yourself that you can't stop, that image will become stronger and stronger.

"Instead, whenever that image comes up, you could say to yourself, 'Oh my gosh, I see my son in the morgue, and I can also picture how happy and excited he was on his fifth birthday.'

"When you look at that positive image, when you linger over it and replay it, adding details to flesh it out, perhaps refreshing your memory with photos you took of the occasion, you begin to see other really good moments in his life, too. When you water those thoughts, they grow. You have the power to bring attention to the memories most meaningful to you."

I caution people not to misunderstand what I'm saying. It is important to tell their stories honestly, without trying to censor the bad parts. Early on, they must retell their story to understand it, to process it. But once they do this, they can put the painful memories into a larger context, rather than isolating them from the whole and repeating them endlessly to themselves. Their loved one's life encompassed far more than just its worst moments. For people who are dealing with traumatic grief, who often wonder why the story keeps coming up over and over in their mind, I explain that they don't have a place in their mind to put it yet. Our mind is like a computer that doesn't haven't a file for it yet. It just floats and gets repeated until we integrate it into our psyche.

The World Outside Our Loss

Sometimes after we have reached acceptance and fully felt our pain, we may need to step outside of it and look at it from another perspective, to see how other people make meaning from their losses. Realizing that you're not alone in pain can be helpful.

Some months after Jan's father died, I could see that she needed to shake things up because she was spiraling inward. When she and I talked, she described the inventory of pain she had been making as part of her effort to accept it rather than try to deny it, but she told me she was tired of thinking about it.

"Perhaps it's time to put down the mirror and pick up the binoculars," I suggested.

She got a glimmer in her eyes. I reminded her that she had told me how sad she was that her father was no longer a part of this world because there was so much more of it he had wanted to see. I explained to her that the world he'd wanted to explore was still here, and perhaps she could allow herself to see some of it.

"I don't know how to do that," she said.

"How about calling a friend and making a date to do something special?" I asked.

"I can't," she said quickly. "I can't. I need to be alone."

It occurred to me that even though she didn't want to be with anyone else yet, perhaps she could see some plays and movies as a way of peering into the lives of others and taking a step back into the world. She seemed to like that idea.

After a month, I checked in on her. She had gone to a number of plays and movies, which had taken her out of herself, and she felt much better for having seen them. But while other people in her position might have done this through laughter, she had made a point of not seeing comedies. She chose instead to see stories about characters who suffered. "It was helpful to be in someone else's pain," she told me. "I sat in theaters and let someone else's love and sorrow wash over me. I was so moved by the art.

"In the theater I saw the tapestry of life. And it helped me to realize I was a player in the great human drama. My loss was heart-wrenching, but I could see that other people's losses were, too. I began to care about the characters in the stories I was watching, to become interested in what happened to them. I felt love. I felt compassion. I found myself laughing at funny moments. Was that me who just laughed? Is that okay? If crying is a part of life, so is laughter. I began to see my life in a more connected way. I felt myself rising back into life. Connecting with myself was important, and so was reconnecting outward to humanity.

"My outer world began to expand. I was intentional about whom I spent my time with, because when I was with them, I was present with my heart and whole being."

For Jan, this is how the pain of her grief began to heal. I do want to offer a word of caution: this choice to look outward was made in her own way and on her own timetable. For many people early in grief is a time to turn completely inward. That's what they need to do, and no amount of urging them to reconnect with the world is going to change that. But as Jan explained to me once she began her journey back to the world, "There's a fine line between fully feeling pain and sitting around sticking knives in the wound. I looked inward, felt the pain, and dug down into it. There was no part of me avoiding it. In fact, I think I was beginning to indulge it. My pain was becoming special. I know that sounds strange, but it was demanding all my attention. My pain seemed to be escalating and I knew I had to do something different. I had to look outward."

Changing the Meaning

How does the search for meaning help those who have endured some of life's worst events? What kinds of stories can they tell themselves that will be true to what they have experienced and also to their healing?

I talked to a colleague, Duane, who works with people who have been through terrible situations that often contain traumatic grief. How does he help them find meaning from such experiences? "I look at the meaning the person is giving the event," he said, "and then I help them change the meaning, not the event. The event is not going to be any different, but the meaning can be, and this can help them to deal with the loss."

Changing the meaning of an event is not easy, and often it's too challenging to do on our own. Sometimes friends can help, sometimes counselors and therapists may be necessary.

I asked Duane for an example from his work. He said:

I remember a horrific story. A woman's daughter had been missing for twenty years and no body was ever found. The rumor in town was that a farmer and his two sons who lived out of town had murdered her, and then fed her to the pigs. The mother had a very strong Christian faith. She sought help, but no one was able to help her. She didn't know for sure whether her daughter was dead, but that was her belief, and she also believed the story about what had happened to her. While we were talking about that horrific image she had been unable to get out of her mind, I said, "I wonder what your daughter thought about when she was watching this happen to her body."

The woman looked at me like I was crazy. "What are you talking about?" she asked.

"If this story is true, your daughter was dead before they cut her up. She would have already arrived in heaven, and I wonder what she was thinking."

That totally changed this woman's perspective, because she had kept picturing her daughter *in the pain* of the moment, feeling excruciating pain. Even as a devout Christian, she had never imagined the possibility that her daughter wasn't in pain at that moment, that she had left her body and was somewhere else. Once she was able to change the meaning of that terrible scene in her mind, it lost its hold on her.

This seems like an extreme example, but it relates to many people in grief. I talk with people who are worried about their loved one's body in the cold weather, snow, or rain. Or they tell me their loved one was claustrophobic and hate the idea of them being buried in the cemetery. These thoughts complicate the grief by adding painful scenarios. Helping them untangle the spirit from the body can be tremendously helpful.

The reality is that no two people will react to an event in the same way. How you respond will depend upon the meaning you see in it. And like all perceptions of meaning, this will be influenced not just by the event itself, but by your cultural background, your family, religion, temperament, and life experience. Meaning comes from all that has made you who you are.

A question that both Duane and I often ask people in traumatic grief is, "Where is your loved one *now*?"

Though the question may seem ridiculous at first, and they don't understand why we ask it, answering it helps them understand that their loved one is no longer in the moment. If they believe in the afterlife, they can imagine their loved one safe in heaven or wherever. If they have no such belief, they can still find comfort in the idea of their loved one being past suffering.

The question of "when" applies to the grieving person as well as to the dead. In my workshops I teach therapists that we put a lot of emphasis on wondering *how* someone is doing in their grief. What if we also asked, "*When* are they?"

To illustrate what I mean, I tell the audience I'm going to make up a story. I then recount in a calm voice that it's strange to be back here again since I was assaulted in this very conference center five years ago. I say, "Wow, I remember it like it was yesterday. I was so afraid for my life. I thought I was going to die."

Then I ask the group, "When am I?"

They respond, "You're now."

"Yes, correct. I am now, remembering five years ago. What if I had come into this room yelling, 'This is a very unsafe room. I was assaulted here five years ago. Keep your eye on the doors. Anyone could get in and attack us!' " My voice is animated and intense. My movements are large and shaky.

"When am I?" I ask the group.

They answer, "Five years ago."

"Yes, correct. I'm feeling the feelings of five years ago today. That is post-traumatic stress." Then I ask the room of therapists, "What would you do to calm me down?"

"I'd ask you to take some deep breaths," someone said.

"Great. Why?"

"To ground you."

Deep breathing grounds me in my body and brings me into this present moment.

Another therapist says, "I'd tell you to name five things in the room."

"Good!" I say, "I see a brown pattern carpet on the floor. I see people sitting in lots of chairs. I see lights in the ceiling and big windows on both sides and doors in the back of the room. That's five things. Why did you just ask me to do that?"

They collectively say that they brought me into the now, the present moment. They helped me go from five years ago to today.

That's what I try to do with those I work with. I want to know, are you still at your loved one's deathbed? Are you still hearing the bad news? Are you still at the funeral? Where are you and when are you?

I want to help grieving people visit the story again, but not get stuck there, perpetually feeling yesterday's feelings today.

In grief, we often entangle the past, present, and future. We need to come into the present moment so we're getting our meaning from the now, not the then. That literally changes our minds and allows us to realize our loved one is no longer dying and in pain. Their suffering is in the past. And their life was far more than just the suffering of their final days.

I help them think about where they are now. They are no longer in the room with their dying loved one. I'm helping them move from their past to the present and eventually to their future. I also ask them what's happened to their loved one since the death. Of course, I don't have an answer, but I want them to think about the questions. Where is their loved one now? What are they doing? Just like Duane, I want them to realize that they and their loved ones have a future past that horrific moment. People will tell me their loved ones are in heaven with God or watching over them or they are learning or helping others in the afterlife.

Trauma expert Janina Fisher tells patients, "You won't feel hope for a long time—hope comes after we begin to feel safer and better." Finding a sense of hope about the future is important in grief, because people continually replaying negative memories signifies that they are stuck in the past.

Allowing yourself only to focus on the past, however miserably, can seem easier, more comfortable, than deciding to live fully in a world without your loved one. The negative can be comforting in its familiarity, while deciding to move forward can be frightening because it makes you feel like you're losing your loved one not once, but twice. It's also scary because it requires you to move into the unknown, into a life that is different without that person. Many of us know someone who lost a loved one and refused to build a new life afterward. They may have held on to their loved one's possessions, turned the loved one's bedroom into a shrine that can never be altered, held fast to all the old routines. At the other extreme they may remove all traces of the loved one's presence. Neither one is healthy. We must move slowly into the unknown of life after death. Underneath the reluctance to live or love again is fear. Pain seems safer. This reminds me of a quote by John A. Shedd: "A ship in harbor is safe, but that's not what ships are built for."

When we are grieving, we want to stay in harbor. It's a good place to be for a while. It's where we refuel, rebuild, repair. But in the same way ships are meant to sail, we are meant to eventually leave our safe harbor, to take the risk of loving again, to find new adventures, to live a life after loss, and maybe even to help another.

The Parable of the Long Spoons

I tell people who feel stuck in grief that the way forward is to help another person in grief. As the Buddha says, if you are a lamp for someone else, it will brighten your path. Those who are stuck will often say, "Wait, you want me to help another person when I can barely tolerate my own pain?" Or "No one else's grief matters. My grief is the only real grief."

I'm not suggesting anything radical. It could be as simple as posting a kind word online to a newly bereaved person or taking a casserole to a grieving family or donating to a charity after a natural disaster. This is for your own sake as much as for the other person as we help them heal.

Marianne Williamson describes a condition that results when a cell malfunctions in our bodies. She says, "A cell forgets its natural function of collaborating with other healthy cells to serve the healthy functioning of the whole and instead decides to go off and do its own thing. This is called cancer, a malignancy in the body or in the mind."

There is something about collaboration for the greater good that is programmed into our DNA. If you've had a year of grief and know how the worst possible pain feels, you also know the comfort of a kind word or a loving gesture. If you can find it in yourself to give to someone else, it will help two people—the recipient of the kindness, and you. It will also help you become unstuck without you even realizing it.

The parable of the long spoons illustrates this point. A person is ushered through the gates of hell where he is surprised to find that they are made of finely wrought gold. They are exquisite, as is the lush green landscape that lies beyond them. He looks at his guide in disbelief. "It's all so beautiful," he says. "The sight of the meadows and mountains. The sounds of the birds singing in the trees and the scent of thousands of flowers. This can't be hell."

When the tantalizing aroma of a gourmet meal catches his attention, he enters a large dining hall. There are rows of tables laden with platters of sumptuous food, but the people seated around the tables are pale and emaciated, moaning in hunger. As he gets closer, he sees that each person is holding a spoon, but the spoon is so long he can't get the food to his mouth. Everyone is screaming and starving in agony.

Now he goes to another area where he encounters the same beauty he witnessed in hell. He sees the same scene in the dining hall with the same long spoons. But here in heaven the people seated at the tables are cheerfully talking and eating because one person is feeding someone sitting across from him.

Heaven and hell offer the same circumstances and conditions. The difference is in the way people treat each other. Choosing to be kind creates one kind of reality. Choosing to be self-centered creates another.

CHAPTER FIVE

The Decision

Doesn't everything die at last, and too soon?
Tell me, what is it you plan to do with your one wild
and precious life?

—Mary Oliver

Each of us has a decision to make about how to heal from a loss. Before you make it, it's important to understand that not making a decision *is* a decision. Healing does not allow for neutrality. It's an active process, not a passive one. Each of us must decide whether or not we want to live again. The decision is a subtle yet most powerful one. Living is different from being alive. We come out of loss alive, but we're not living yet.

I was fortunate to spend a little time with Mother Teresa at her Home for the Dying Destitute in India the year before she died. Although she was old and frail, she seemed like the happiest person I had ever met. She told me, "Life is an achievement." When I point that out to people who are feeling helpless, they begin to understand that they can find strength and meaning by making a conscious decision to continue to live. When people show up at my grief support groups, I tell them I'm there to help them grieve and to help them live. I thank them for coming and tell them I know how much courage it must have taken for them simply to walk in the door. They'll tell me, "But I hurt so much, and life is so hard." I remind them that finding meaning will help them deal with the pain and that meaning is everywhere.

In response to deep pain, we have the freedom to make a decision about how we're going to live. Viktor Frankl writes about watching his fellow inmates in the concentration camp respond in different ways to the terrible conditions of their lives. Given the horror of their circumstances, it might have seemed that there was no room for any kind of freedom of choice, and certainly not for any kind of joy. And yet there was. Writing about a journey from one camp to another that he and his fellow prisoners were sent on, he says: "If someone had seen our faces on the journey from Auschwitz to a Bavarian camp as we beheld the mountains of Salzburg with their summits glowing in the sunset, through the little barred windows of the prison carriage, he would never have believed that those were the faces of men who had given up all hope of life and liberty. Despite that factor—or maybe because of it—we were carried away by nature's beauty."

The decision to live fully is about being present for life, no matter how hard life is at the moment. It's about what you are made of, not what happens to you.

I knew I needed to make that decision after the death of my son—to cast a vote for life to continue. There are many ways of doing that, and my going back to work within a couple of months of his death was one tentative step in that direction. There have been many others in the time since then. One day I posted a random picture of myself on Facebook. It was like announcing that I had come back to work, and people said how relieved they were to see that I was okay.

Six months after David died, our sweet old dog, Angel, died. Our world felt empty. A year after Angel's death, we decided to get a puppy. I was hyperaware that I was choosing a sweet dog to love, and that chances were she would be leaving me in about fifteen years. In the midst of my painful, forced separation from my son, David, and my dog, Angel, I was choosing to attach again, even though I knew it would result in loss. I could have avoided it. I didn't have to get a dog again. But I purposely made a decision to bring love back into my home.

There had been so much subtraction, it seemed time for some addition. Surprisingly, loss is optional. If I want a life with no loss, I also get a life with no love, no spouse or partner, no children, no friends, and no pets. Avoiding the prospect of loss also means avoiding the joys of life. C. S. Lewis said in his book *The Problem of Pain*, "Try to exclude the possibility of suffering which the order of nature and the existence of free wills involve, and you find that you have excluded life itself."

Each day after David died, I saw life going on around me—and in me, too. My hair continued to grow, my fingernails and toenails did, too, and my heart was still beating. I decided that it must be for a reason, and that I should make a conscious decision to live, not just be alive. Now, sometimes when I'm doing a workshop and someone tells me they're not sure why they're still here, I will gently take their hand and feel their pulse. Yes, you're still alive, I say, so what's it going to be? Live or not live? Most realize that question has to be answered.

Writing this book has been part of my decision to return to life. I've had many moments when I thought I have to find a way to live again, most of all for the integrity of my life, but also for the integrity of the book.

Many readers will think, "It's too late for me. I'm past the point of being able to live again." There is a Chinese proverb that asks the question, "When is the best time to plant a tree?" The answer is twenty years ago. When is the second-best time? Now. People say to me, "I'm trying." I tell them, "There is no trying. Living again is a decision. It's also a declaration. The intent precedes the action and the result."

Years before we knew how to make it happen, President Kennedy said we would go to the moon. Louise Hay talked about the importance of our words to create actions. You can't just wake up and see if today is the day you'll act. Yoda from *Star Wars* was correct: "Do or do not, there is no try." Even a small decision makes a difference.

Learned Helplessness

Yet sometimes help just feels out of reach. On my Facebook page, a woman posted about her son who had died. She said it had been four painful years and she hadn't been able to find help. "This is always the case," she added. "Even as a young girl when bad things happened, I never got any help."

I didn't know if she was just sharing her experience or looking for help, so I asked her.

She responded with, "The pain is unbearable, nothing will help."

"What city do you live in?" I was afraid it was a small city with no resources. But she responded that she lived in a major city. I sent a link and told her, "This is from Grief.com and there are some free support groups in your area."

She wrote back, "I'm not a group person."

"I got it," I said, "so here's a link to counselors in your area."

"I can't go out."

"Are you physically challenged?" I asked.

"No, the grief is just too much to bear."

"You never leave the house?"

"Just for work, groceries, and sometimes Starbucks."

"I have an online workshop and group that may help you," I told her. "Let's private message each other the details."

In a message she wrote, "If there is a cost, I can't afford to pay for it."

"I'm happy to give it to you if you can't afford it."

She agreed, and I asked for her email to get started in my online workshop and group.

"I don't give out my email address. I don't like giving out identifying information."

I said, "Isn't that what an email is for, so we don't have to give out identifying information?"

"I don't give it out."

I realized I had done everything in my power to help, and now it was up to her. I can't force help on anyone.

I never know for sure what's going on in these situations, but I see that the wounds of the past stop us from getting help in the present. They register in us as helplessness. When I share this concept with people in grief and they see how much compassion I have for them, they soften. Many times they want to know more about how their past has contributed to their being stuck in grief.

To understand this, let's look at some experiments from the 1960s that focused on the phenomenon of *learned helplessness*. As an animal lover, I don't condone these experiments and I hope they wouldn't be done today. Nevertheless, the results reveal how our past wounds continue to affect us. Psychologists divided dogs into three different groups:

Group One—The dogs were given shocks and there was no way to avoid them.
Group Two—The dogs were given shocks, which they could avoid by pressing a button with their noses.
Group Three—The dogs received no shocks.

Once they had completed this first experimental manipulation, all the dogs were placed one at a time in a box with two chambers that were separated by a low barrier, and all of them were given shocks. Group-one dogs just took the shock and never jumped over the barrier into the second chamber to try to escape the shocks. They had been conditioned to be helpless and take the shocks. But the dogs in groups two and three jumped over the barrier. Nothing had taught them that they had to suffer passively.

This phenomenon can also be seen in the way elephants are trained. When an elephant is still a baby, the trainer uses a rope to tie one of the elephant's legs to a post. The baby elephant struggles for hours, or sometimes even days, trying to escape the rope. Eventually the animal quiets down and accepts its limited range of motion. When the elephant grows up, it'll clearly be strong enough to break the rope, but because by then it has learned that struggling is useless, and it will no longer attempt to break the rope.

Many people grew up in horrible situations and weren't able to get the help they needed. Their painful childhoods turned into challenging adulthoods. They were left believing that when loss came to their world, they could never survive it.

The reality is that there is something they can do. How did scientists help the dogs in group one move to the shock-free side? They needed a slight push to learn. Small steps are what's needed. For example, someone told me about her grieving sister after the loss of a spouse. "It's been two years. She never leaves the house. She won't go out, says nothing will help."

I asked, "What have you told her to do?"

"Get a job, go volunteer, or take a trip!"

I said, "If she is rarely leaving the house, those sound like big things. What if one week you brought over a coffee and just visited? Try that for a few weeks, then perhaps say, 'Let's go out for a coffee.' When we have learned helplessness, big steps are too much. We must help with small, incremental steps."

As a griever, after months or maybe even years of wondering how anything can ever be meaningful after the loss you experienced, you may gradually start to notice that you are deciding to live again in small steps. It may manifest in subtle ways. You don't suddenly start to date again or go to parties, but you're shocked to discover that you still enjoy the taste of a great espresso, or that you want to take a long walk in the park with your best friend. Little by little, you start caring again about things, both large and small.

It's important for people to understand for a few people, the decision may occur in a moment, but for most, it's a process. If I were to ask someone if they've decided to live again when they're still waiting for the autopsy report, that would be far too soon. Over time, however, they can begin to ponder the question.

Norma, who was in her fifties, was making dinner with her husband when he had a sudden heart attack. He fell to the floor and she called the paramedics, but he had died instantly. Over the next year, she was so shocked and bereft she wasn't sure she wanted to go on living. We had several talks in which she shared the depth of pain she was feeling. She said, "I don't know what I'm supposed to do next."

"Have you decided whether you want to live or not?" I asked her.

"I haven't made that decision yet," she told me.

I encouraged her to pay attention to her body, her actions, and the world around her. I asked her to notice if things were moving forward.

"What things?" she asked.

"Everything. Your digestive tract. The cars on the road. The wind blowing."

She called me later and said, "David, I get it. Everything is alive and moving but me. I can collect cobwebs, or I can move with the flow. My moving again won't make my husband's death go away and it doesn't mean I'm going to forget him. But I want to quit fighting the wind."

Norma realized that, for her, not making a decision felt like resisting the natural order of things. She made a decision to stop fighting it.

Disloyalty

Norma's declaration that returning to life wouldn't mean forgetting her husband brings up another issue, one that I often see in people who were married or people who were in long-term relationships. They are concerned about starting to date again or doing anything that would translate to being disloyal to their loved one. There's an unspoken belief that to enjoy life after the death of someone dear to them will mean that they didn't really love that person.

I believe that this uneasiness comes in part from the fact that for most of us, there is no defined period of mourning. Back in the days when you wore black for a year, you knew that at the end of that year you had given full due to your loss and could now throw off your "widow's weeds" (or the equivalent) and be given permission to reenter life. There was no sense that this would equate with disloyalty to the deceased. Whenever I hear someone who is concerned about disloyalty, I gently tell them that their marriage vows were to last "till death do us part." The marriage contract ends at death. It is done. No one's vows include the afterlife.

Sometimes it has even been the spouse who has paved the way for this return to life and love. Years ago I worked at a hospice where a woman named Marjorie was sitting with her dying husband, Luke. "I don't know what I'm going to do after you're gone," she told him. "I don't know how I'll live again." He said to her, "Miss me, but love again." "How can I love again? I don't know what to do with all this love I have for you." "Spread it around," he said. "Give it to your friends and family. If you meet another man, give it to him. It was my honor to have it for this long and I'll take a part of it with me."

My nephew, Jeffrey, was a well-loved TV comedy writer. He and his wife wrote for successful shows like *The Nanny* and *Third Rock from the Sun*. When he was in his forties, he was diagnosed with leukemia. He fought cancer with his wit and wisdom. When the medical team was getting him ready for a bone marrow procedure, he had a massive brain bleed and died. His death was quite unexpected, since he'd been doing so well. And yet, he'd prepared for it.

After his death, his wife was going through his things and found a letter he had written to her just in case something went wrong. He knew that at some point the question of her dating again would have to come up and he wanted to make sure she knew his views on this. He wrote:

My love, this will sound crazy in light of what's happened,
but you should do whatever you need to be happy in this life.
Despite what you may think, you deserve to be happy. If you
find someone else to be with someday, no matter who it is,
if they make you happy that's what I want for you. You still
have your whole life ahead of you. Make the most of it. I did.

Love forever,
Jeffrey

Of course not everyone who loses someone they loved deeply will believe they have been given this kind of permission. When two people are in love, it can be difficult for either of them to imagine their sweetheart in love with someone else. The fiancée of a friend of mine was killed in a car accident when she was twenty-two. He was twenty-four, in deep grief, and he swore he would never love again. He spent the next few years mourning her death.

He asked me to lunch one day and said, "I've never loved anyone the way I loved Shannon. But in a couple of years, I'm going to be thirty. I've been wondering if I'm prepared to spend the rest of my life alone."

I asked him what he thought Shannon would have wanted.

"She would have hated the idea of my being with someone else."

This was not what I expected to hear. But after a minute I said, "Do you believe in an afterlife?"

"Yes," he said.

"Your grief has brought you a lot of wisdom. When I asked you what Shannon would want, you thought about that sweet, innocent, twenty-two-year-old girl. I believe that her death has matured you and made you wiser. And I have to believe it has done the same for her. A wiser Shannon in the afterlife might say something completely different now. Wherever she is and whatever she's doing, I'm sure you wish her love. And why wouldn't you expect the same kind of generosity from her?"

Another reason for being reluctant to live again is that we don't want the finality of a goodbye. Sometimes we need help making the decision to say our goodbyes to them in life and move our loved ones into our hearts in death.

A woman in one of my retreats was grieving the death of her fiancé, Evan, who had died during the war in Afghanistan. She told me it was the anniversary of their engagement that night.

"Earlier in the day," Tina said, "I went to my safe-deposit box at the bank to get my engagement ring. It's been nine years since he died, but there are moments, like today, when I'm still in the throes of my grief for him. There are times when it feels like it's hitting me like a brick."

I asked her what her goal was at the retreat.

"To find peace and fully grieve Evan, so I can move forward."

"What would you like to have in your life now?"

"Love," she replied. "I want to fall in love again. I don't understand what the problem is. It's been nine years. But I just can't seem to forget Evan."

"Tina," I said gently. "You don't need to forget Evan in order to make room in your life for someone else. It's not about forgetting him. But you do need to let him go."

"What makes you think I haven't let him go?"

"Tina, at the same time that you're telling me you want to find love, you're also telling me you went to your safe-deposit box today to retrieve your engagement ring. Doesn't that suggest that you're still holding on to the past?"

Tina laughed, but countered: "What does that have to do with my love life now?"

"Don't you think that that ring represents a connection that might get in the way of forming a relationship with a new man?"

"I just tried on a ring, that's all. I don't usually wear it. I have a hope chest of his things, like his uniform, his medals, a yellow ribbon, and some journals that I kept while he was gone. I put the chest in the attic, since I knew it wouldn't be a great thing to have it in my bedroom if I decided to bring another man into my life. But the flag is still in my living room."

"What flag?"

"The flag from his casket," she replied. "I like to think that I can find a balance between remembering Evan and creating another life for myself."

"Tina, I have great respect for Evan and the sacrifice he made for his country. And I certainly understand your desire to honor him for it. My mother also had a flag on her casket, because she served in the Coast Guard. It's in my closet with a few other special possessions from her life that I really treasure. Her memory occupies space in my heart but, except for a couple of photos of her, not in my living room. You've created space to honor Evan's death front and center in your living room. There's nothing wrong with that. But if you want another man to occupy that space someday, you might consider how that would make him feel."

"What am I supposed to do?"

"I don't want you to get rid of the flag from Evan's casket, but you could move it to a much less conspicuous place. Somewhere that wouldn't make a date feel as though he was intruding on another deceased soldier's turf. Or you could just put it in the chest with all your other memorabilia and take it out every once in a while when you are really missing him."

She said, "That's interesting. I'll think about that."

"One more thing," I said. "If the roles were reversed and it was you who had died, what advice would you give Evan if he had your flag in his living room and had invited a date over for dinner?"

"I would say he should give the girl a fighting chance! Move the flag. It's not me. You can remember me without having to see me every day." She looked down. "Okay, okay, maybe I'm still hanging on a little."

Tina, like everyone who is in mourning, has many layers of acceptance to move through. If she had come to me sometime in the first year or two after losing Evan, I would never have told her to move memorabilia that related to him to a less prominent place in her home. However, when we spoke it was nine years after Evan's death, and she was clear about the fact that she wanted to find love again. I don't think Evan would have wanted to sentence Tina to years of loneliness. Although I'm sure he would want to be remembered, as all of us hope we will be, that needn't mean that she can't find space in her heart—and her home—for another man.

No matter how long you were together, it's not enough time, but the love you shared is not gone. It lives within you, as a part of you. The experience of love that you had can never be destroyed or changed by a new love. That love will exist forever in its own time, in its own way, in your heart. But more love can be available to you if you desire. Your heart can have many loves in its lifetime. A new love can grow out of the same soil without diminishing a past love. You still have a life. It was one you didn't prepare for and you didn't want. But this road is still worth traveling. Your story is still in the making, waiting for you to find it.

My hope is that all your experiences of the past, all the love you had, will pave the way for you to find that new story. Whether you find other companions for the journey or choose to go it alone is entirely up to you. Both can be wonderfully fulfilling. But if you want a new love, as Tina did, it's up to you to be open to it, so that when it appears, you will welcome it.

At times, our challenge is a new love; other times it is a new life. A man in his late forties told me after a lecture, "My family wanted me to talk to you. I haven't cared about living since my wife died five years ago."

I asked for an example of what he meant.

"I don't care about going to family weddings. I don't care what's going on with the kids or the grandkids."

"Would your wife have cared about the children or the weddings?"

"Oh yes."

"What would she have thought about your decision not to engage with anyone in your life? Your decision not to live?"

That stopped him. "No, I didn't make that decision!"

I asked him to think about the reality that on some level he did.

We often don't realize that the decision to live is an active one that requires our participation. There will be a period when it's too painful to consider life again. Then there comes a time when, coasting along, we're almost shocked to notice that life does continue. All around us it's happening. That's when we must actively decide whether to join it. We're capable of more love throughout our lives than we realize.

As a bereaved parent, I, too, have wrestled with the concept of disloyalty. After David's death, I only allowed myself to laugh after telling a funny story about him. A smile or a laugh felt okay if it was connected to him, but not otherwise. I don't remember exactly when it happened or what it was about, but at a certain point, I just laughed at something. I was startled, because it was the first time my laughter didn't relate to David, and I was immediately flooded with tears and self-judgment. What kind of parent was I to be able to laugh again when my son was dead? I could not have imagined that this was possible, and now that I'd done it, I didn't think it was right.

I sat in that lost place for a while. Life continued around me. Focusing on others helped. My other son, Richard, still deserved to smile. The young kids in my family still looked for a laugh when they did something funny. Day by day, I had to beat down the belief that living again was a dishonor to my son who had died. I had to create a new image in my mind of what loyalty to David would look like. Loyalty would mean a full life, not ever forgetting, but putting his love into everything I did and everything I am.

The Shattered Vase

Stephen Joseph is a psychologist and professor in the School of Education at the University of Nottingham in the UK. He tells a story he calls "The Shattered Vase." "What if you accidentally break a treasured vase into small pieces?" he asked. "What do you do? You have a choice to try to put the vase back together, but it will never be the same. The other choice is to pick up the beautiful colored pieces and use them to make something new. Perhaps a colorful mosaic heart could be created."

What do you do after the familiar life you loved gets broken, just like that vase? You can try to put your life back together exactly as it was, but it will remain fractured, vulnerable. Those who accept the breakage and build themselves anew become more resilient and open to new ways of living. I remind people that *broken crayons can still color*, and while our lives may feel broken, we still have the potential to create something beautiful.

A lyric from the song "Pompeii," by the English indie rock band Bastille, says, "How am I going to be an optimist about this?" I thought about that after David's death. That is one of the big questions.

I'm not asking you to be an optimist about what happened. I'm not asking you to see the glass half full. There is nothing half full about your loved one dying. I'm asking you to be optimistic about your future, to hope that you can still create a life worth living. If you're reading this book, you're probably not there yet. I wasn't there when I started writing it. But the fact that you *are* reading this book is a small statement of hope.

After David died, I could not find my footing. It was as though I was no longer on solid ground and I felt myself falling, falling, into a bottomless pit of pain. But I had learned a lot from the losses of my mother and father as well as the countless people in grief with whom I've had the privilege of sitting. I understood that that pit of pain could become the place into which I could pour the concrete for a new foundation in my life—a foundation on which I would be able to stand in the future. I can't undo what happened. David's death will never be okay, and I'm never going to forget David. That's not going to happen. But I am hopeful about what I can make of my life in the future, and that is my form of optimism.

Part II

Challenges in Grief

CHAPTER SIX

Finding Meaning in *Why*

New beginnings are often disguised as painful endings.
—Lao-tzu

There are many variations of the *haunting Why question*: Why did my child die? Why was my loved one murdered? Why did my husband die in a car accident the day after we got married? Why did tragedy strike us? Why him? Why her? Why them? There must be a reason. Life can't be that cruel and random.

Many people spend years looking for a why answer that will never come. There is no satisfying answer to why your loved one cheated on you. Or divorced you. Or died. But finding meaning is still possible. You can find meaning in why your loved one *lived*. What did your loved one get out of being here? And what did you get out of knowing him or her? Did anything good come from the relationship? Did anything good come out of the death?

People often have a knee-jerk reaction to that question, assuring me that no good could possibly come of their loss. But it can. Perhaps you are a more compassionate person now. Perhaps the tragedy helped change the way you deal with other people who have suffered losses. Maybe your loved one's death shed a public light on violence or brought attention to a deadly disease. Even in the worst tragedies, people are often surprised to find some good.

There's also the *why me* question, which I hear a lot in my work with grieving people. The answer may be hard to hear.

In my workshops, we don't deal with this until the second day because the answer *is* so challenging. I guide people gently into it. I begin by asking each person in the room to state something bad that has happened in his or her life. It may not be the loss that brought them there. It could be something else. All kinds of answers arise. One person tells about being bullied, the next person about being raped. Someone's brother died when he was young. Someone else's house just burned down. A person was molested as a child. Another had an alcoholic father or a bipolar mother. The litany of losses and griefs goes on and includes everything from death to betrayal, miscarriage to chronic disease.

After we go around the room, I say, "Everyone has something. My guess is that many of you have more than one thing. Does anyone have nothing? Is there anyone here whose life has been perfect? No loss? No pain?"

No hands go up.

"So no one has had a perfect past," I continue. "Do any of you foresee a future without pain or loss?"

Still no hands.

Then I ask them what they got out of hearing about other people's losses. Did it affect their question of *why me*? Someone will say some version of, "I guess the real question is, Why not me? Why did I think I was going to get through this life without sorrow, pain, or grief?"

That's the deal in this life, the good and the bad. No one gets just the good.

Our work is to live with the questions and find meaning in the tragedy. In chapter 1, I wrote about being afraid I would crash the plane after my mother died. It's not surprising that later in my career I tried to make meaning from that fear by doing volunteer work with the Red Cross aviation disaster team. My first experience came in 2000, after a Singapore Airlines 747 taxied down a runway that was under construction, hit a bulldozer, and burst into flames. Nearly one hundred of the passengers were burned alive.

In any plane disaster, there are usually three locations where help is provided:

1. The plane's departure point
2. The plane's intended arrival point
3. The crash site

I was assigned to the intended arrival point, Los Angeles International Airport (LAX), where the plane had been headed and where family members would be waiting for their loved ones to arrive. In the first hours, we didn't know who had survived, and the uncertainty was excruciating. This is always extremely challenging, since TV news often airs live developing stories faster than the airlines can distribute information. The only part that does not come out live are the names of those on the plane.

Once the survivors had been identified, it was our task to support those who learned that their loved ones had died. In these situations people scream, pass out, and fall to their knees, and it is our job to keep them safe. One person's pain has a ripple effect on everyone else in the area. It is a deeply human moment that I as a first responder can only be present for. "Here is some water, let's sit down," I say as I do what I can to ground them. I gently tell them about possible reactions to such an event. Connection is the next step. Connections to ongoing resources, people they know. When they're ready, we ask, "Who do you need to call? Who can we call to support you through this tragedy?"

We also reached out to support those passengers who had survived and rebooked to fly to LAX, many of whom were still reeling from the ordeal they had been through. I met with a number of the survivors of that flight. One businessman, Dan, stands out in my memory. I greeted him as he disembarked. His car was at the airport, so no one was meeting him. I talked to him for a few minutes, describing the reactions he might have once his initial shock had worn off, and offering him resources for how to deal with them. I told him there were some private exits he could use at LAX to avoid the media. He didn't understand why the media would have any interest in him. I explained that on all the TV networks there had been footage of the plane on fire and everyone had been horrified by the images and the thought of people dying in those flames.

"They're interested in me because I was a witness?" he asked.

"That's part of it," I said.

"What else would they care about?"

"You lived!" I said. "You're news because you lived."

While living through a disaster is certainly remarkable, the mere fact of being alive is remarkable, too, "an achievement," as Mother Teresa had told me. When I ask people why they woke up this morning, they have no idea why I would want to know. But they dutifully go through the motions of telling me that the alarm clock woke them, or the sun, or the dog that jumped on their bed. I then remind them that although the sun rose this morning, many people didn't wake up to see it. Though alarms went off in houses all over the world, there were people who didn't hear them because they were dead. Some dogs jumped on beds to find that their owners had died. You didn't just *happen* to wake up this morning, I tell them. You woke up for a reason, and that reason is *for the purpose of finding meaning* in your life.

Few of us take the time to explore what meaning we can create. Of course, if you discover the polio vaccine, the meaning of your life is obvious. But most of us don't have such newsworthy contributions to make. One man who did was Jonas Salk, the American medical researcher and virologist who discovered and developed one of the first successful polio vaccines. When I was young, I saw a newsreel about Salk's work in which a reporter said to him, "When you patent this, you'll become the richest man in the world."

"It's not mine to patent," Salk replied. "It belongs to all of humanity."

I was so struck that he had made such an amazing breakthrough and then chose to give it all away. How magnanimous and heroic. I hoped that someday, somehow, such a huge opportunity would be offered to me and I could show that I was as big a man as Jonas Salk.

Twenty years later I was in Washington, DC, and I was asked to serve on a health care committee. I had no idea who the other members would be. When we all converged around a large table, I saw an older gentleman who looked familiar. The name card in front of him read Jonas Salk. I couldn't believe it. I couldn't wait to see this larger-than-life man in action.

During the long meeting, I felt like we were deep in the weeds because there were so many health care issues at stake. I wanted to tackle the big stuff first. But as I watched this man of whom I was in so much awe, I saw that he was completely dedicated to working out every small detail involved in making recommendations about these large issues. Suddenly, the reality of one of my character flaws hit me. I was always hoping for the big moment when I could really show up. He, on the other hand, was present for the small moments as well as the big ones.

When you consider how to find meaning in your life, you probably think only the big moments count. But they *all* do. Whether you're donating a million dollars to a worthy cause or saying a kind word to the checkout person at the grocery store, volunteering at the local soup kitchen, or just being considerate to the driver trying to enter the lane in front of you, everything you do has the potential for meaning.

I remember a meeting I went to with my son, David, when he needed health insurance. I'd made the plan for the meeting even though he was totally uninterested in getting insurance. This just wasn't something he thought was important. Because he'd resisted going, I imagined a tense meeting where he would roll his eyes at every suggestion the agent threw out. But that isn't how the meeting went.

The insurance agent wasn't anyone I knew—just someone whose name I'd pulled from a local listing—so I had no idea what to expect. It turned out she wasn't like any insurance agent I'd ever imagined. When Tally entered the room, it was as if she had just walked on stage. With short blond hair that had a pink streak running through it, she looked far too hip to be selling insurance. She was funny, sarcastic, and a bit irreverent. But she was not putting forth any special effort. For her, this was just another business meeting, we were just two of her many clients, and she was simply being herself. Because of who she was and how she interacted with David, however, what could have been a stressful, unpleasant meeting turned out fine. At the end of the meeting, David reached out and shook her hand to thank her and we walked out, both of us happy that he now had health insurance. We hugged goodbye. That meeting was the last time I would ever see David alive.

Tally will forever be meaningful in my life. She helped create a memory that I will always cherish. She didn't know that this would be the last encounter I would have with my son. She wasn't trying to create a big moment, but as it turned out, because of her, a completely routine meeting became something that will forever mean the world to me. That is how life works. We affect others in ways we will never know, often by simply being ourselves.

Survivor's Guilt

When someone has survivor's guilt, they may believe that they should be dead and the loved one should be alive—perhaps because the person died while doing something the survivor was supposed to do. It may be that the survivor thinks they could have done something to prevent the death. Or maybe the person who died was young and the survivor is old and feels that he or she should have gone first in the natural order of things. Whatever the reason, when there's guilt, there's a demand for punishment, so survivors will often punish themselves or attract people who will do it for them.

During one of my weekend retreats for people in grief at Esalen in Northern California, I invited a woman to come up to the front of the room to do some healing work. She asked if her husband could join her. It can be tricky to work with two grieving people, but I sensed it was the right thing to do.

When Joe and Sandra sat beside me, I asked what had brought them there. Sandra said her twenty-four-year-old son had been killed on his motorcycle by an elderly man who had hit the gas pedal instead of the brake.

I felt her pain. I saw her heartbreak and suffering, and I asked her, "In all this tragedy, what's your worst thought?"

She said, "It's my fault."

"Why?" I asked.

"I wanted to tell him not to ride that motorcycle. It was too dangerous. I even told Joe that I was going to stop him, and he said, 'You can't.' But I could have. I could have saved his life."

"What happened to the driver?" I asked.

"He lost his license and was put on probation."

"What's your response to that?"

"He's in his eighties. I can't blame him. He's just an old man who made a mistake."

"You could blame him," I said. I turned to her husband and asked, "What do you think of this?"

He said, "It was a terrible tragedy. I'm devastated, but I'm not going to blame him or my wife or myself."

I turned to Sandra and said, "Someone has to pay."

She shot a quick look at me and said, "That's right, someone must pay."

"And that's you?" I asked.

"Yes, that's me. It's my fault," she said through her tears.

"So you put yourself in jail?"

She looked down. "Yes."

"How often have you judged yourself guilty?"

"Daily," she answered.

"Only daily? Isn't it a story you repeat all the time at this point?"

"Yes, okay, a lot, sometimes hourly," she said.

I grabbed her hand. "Let's look at this from a couple of different viewpoints. Did you have a trial?"

"What?"

"Did you have a trial?"

"I don't understand."

"Did you have a trial to see if you were guilty. or did you just walk into jail and throw away the key?"

"I put myself here. I'm guilty."

"I see people in your situation all the time," I said. "Your story is, if I hadn't let him ride his motorcycle, he would still be alive. Did you have control? Did he always listen to you?"

"No."

"You could have said all those things and he might have done it anyway. Right?"

She nodded.

"I've seen people interfere with a situation that did change the circumstances," I told her, "They took the bike away and guess what? Their son took the bus and the bus was hit by a car. They think if they hadn't gotten involved, their child would be alive."

I began to choke up and put my hand on Sandra's back. "I'm sorry your son died," I told her. "I see people who did everything right and their child still died. Now he's gone. It's a tragic reality." Tears were pouring down my face as well as so many other faces in the room.

At this time, my son was still alive, so it wasn't a matter of her pain stirring up my own. But if I'm truly present for another's pain, it becomes tangible. It's in the room.

"I feel your grief. I'm so, so sorry for him and for both of you." I looked into her eyes and said, "But it wasn't your fault."

Joe was nodding in agreement.

I turned to the several hundred people who were watching this unfold. "This is a jury of your peers," I told her. "They've heard the story. Is it her fault?" I asked them.

They yelled out a loud, "No."

"Did you hear that?" I asked her.

"Yes."

"We, the jury, have reviewed your case," I said, "and find that you have been wrongly convicted. Today you can be released. Do you want out of jail?"

"Yes. But my therapist said I could stay in here as long as I need to."

"Do you still need to stay in there now that we've all found you innocent?"

She looked at everyone. "No, I can leave."

"Then step out if you want," I said.

She got off her stool and leaned into my arms, crying. Her husband walked over and gently embraced her.

"Are you ready to take her home from jail?" I asked Joe.

"Yes," he said.

"You will always be connected to your son," I reminded them. "But you don't have to connect in pain. You can connect in love."

As her husband took her back to her seat, I realized that the story she'd been telling herself had been deeply grooved in her mind, and therefore that it was likely to come back if she didn't actively resist it. Part of the reason for its stubborn persistence is that it had become embedded in her mind through frequency of repetition. When your friends and family tell you to quit blaming yourself and you say you can't, it may be true. In 1949, Canadian neuropsychologist Donald Hebb first suggested the idea often paraphrased as, "Neurons that fire together, wire together." The more frequently they fire, the stronger the message they are communicating becomes. I like to use a common analogy to explain this: our brain has pathways that are like a path in the woods. The more we walk along the path, the wider and deeper it becomes, the easier to see, and the more familiar it will feel to us. It becomes the path of least resistance, the preferred path, the one we follow automatically. Our path in grief all too often leads us, as it did Sandra, to "It's my fault" (or "It's his fault").

The other reason we end up there is something I've touched

on before—our need to make sense out of the events of our lives. We are biologically wired to identify patterns, connections, and cause and effect—in other words, to tell ourselves stories. It's how we have survived. If we didn't have a sense of cause and effect, we wouldn't have known to avoid the next lion we saw after the one that killed our friend. Stories give a shape to what might otherwise feel random, and randomness is very hard for us to accept. When something big happens, like the loss of a loved one, there has to be a reason for it, not just chance. We create stories around those events that make sense of the unfathomable—even if those stories are hurtful and self-destructive.

Playing God

When we don't have a *why*, we tend to jump in and play God. We tell ourselves, "I could have prevented his death," or "It should have been me." This means we are attributing to ourselves a power that we don't have. We don't get to decide who lives and who dies.

Archie's wife, Stella, had died of cancer about a year earlier. Although he was still deep in grief when we met, he didn't seem to have any bitterness or survivor's guilt. The story he told me was that when they met and fell in love, Stella had a wonderful son, Jake, from her first marriage. After they got married, Archie and Stella had another child together, Nick. During her pregnancy with Nick, Stella found a lump in her breast. Her doctor told her it wasn't unusual to have swollen glands in preparation for breast-feeding, and she felt reassured. Although they hadn't planned on having another child so soon after Nick, shortly after he was born Stella became pregnant again. And again she found a lump in her breast, which the doctor reassured her was normal during pregnancy. Their second son, Tyler, was born, and all seemed well. Jake loved his two younger brothers, and Archie and Stella felt their family was now complete.

Soon after, however, Stella had a checkup, and test results revealed that the lump had been cancer all along. She had stage IV cancer. She and her family had a strong faith in God and they believed that she would be healed. But after a few years of multiple rounds of chemotherapy, it was clear that her life was winding down. One evening toward the end three-year-old Tyler climbed into bed with his parents. As Stella gently stroked his hair, Archie told her that a coworker of his had said that God really got this one wrong. Stella looked up at him and said, "We can't play God."

After Tyler fell asleep, Archie said, "Honey, if I'd pushed you to get this checked sooner, you'd be healthy now."

Stella looked at him and said, "All I know is that if I had been checked for cancer and it was found, I'd have had chemo and wouldn't have been able to have kids after that. Sweet Tyler wouldn't be here now, and neither would Nick."

Archie agreed, but he still wished she had gotten the lump checked sooner. Stella grabbed his hand and said, "Sweetheart, nothing in me regrets having done what I did, because the result is we have these two children. I'm telling you this because I don't want any of you to feel guilty later. Or blame God. I don't know how God figures out who lives or who dies. Or if it's random and God is there with us in the randomness. I do want you to know that it means the world to me that if I have to leave, I leave knowing that my boys will have each other for their whole lives, and you will have them."

Stella's wise words helped Archie avoid both survivor's guilt and God blaming. To begin to heal, you must give the power back to God, the universe, fate, or whatever you believe in. That might mean you begin to acknowledge your anger at God. I believe that God is big enough to handle your anger and rage. You may have to talk to a spiritual leader, scream in the car, do grief yoga, pound on a pillow, find some other form of emotional and physical release. When you do begin to release some of that anger, you start to recognize that if your loved one died, and you didn't, it was *not supposed* to be you.

How do you know? Because if it was supposed to be you, it would have been. Since you are alive, you need to think about what you intend to do with that life. The *why* you must answer is not why your loved one died, but why you lived. Why are you here? What meaning can you bring to the rest of your life? What meaning can you find in those who are living?

No Useful Moves

I often play solitaire on my phone. When I lose, I want to figure out why, so I hit a button that says, "Replay this game," which presents me with the exact hand of cards I just played. Then I can examine the cards for hints about other moves I could have made that would have given me a better result. But sometimes I discover that given the hand I'd been dealt, even if I played every move exactly right, I would still lose. Then I get the message, "No useful moves could have been played."

This could also be a message about the what-ifs we so often feel in grief. When we find ourselves thinking that if we had done things differently, our loved one would still be here, "No useful moves could have been played" is a reminder that that particular hand has already been played and it is futile to keep reviewing it. The useful moves that remain to us are those that will bring what we have learned from the past into the present and the future. It's up to us to help them make the moves that will bring them into meaning.

The moves of the past have been played, but for the survivor, the future has many possibilities. When I work with someone suffering from survivor's guilt, I often begin with the little moments. The survivor thinks, "I should be the dead one." I bring them into this moment and say, "But you can see you're still here. This moment when you and I are connecting and talking about your pain has meaning. Sharing your pain always has meaning."

There is no making sense of the death, but I help them find a little control in their *why* question.

I ask them these questions:

- How can you honor your loved one?
- How can you create a different life that includes them?
- How can you use your experience to help others?

It is in your control to find meaning every day. You can still love, laugh, grow, pray, smile, cry, live, give, be grateful, be present. You can take the other moments as they come. That can be the meaning. In the end, no matter how hard it is, if we allow ourselves to spend time searching for the meaning in our loss, it will appear because of our search and the healing will happen.

What do we do, however, when we can't see the meaning? In the lyrics to "Wait for It," one of the many wonderful songs in *Hamilton*, Lin-Manuel Miranda reminds us that death will come for all of us, but until it does, we just keep living, and there must be a reason we are still alive. "When everyone who loves me has died / I'm willing to wait for it."

We may not know *why* a loved one died and we remain, but that is the reality. The life that was lost was precious. If we have been granted more time, shouldn't we believe that our life is also precious?

CHAPTER SEVEN

Suicide

Suicide is not a blot on anyone's name; it is a tragedy.
—Kay Redfield Jamison

Never is the torment of self-blaming more acute, or the if-only thoughts more tormenting, than in the aftermath of a death by suicide. We don't talk much about suicide if it's something that has affected us personally. Too painful, too taboo, too laden with unresolved feelings. If we do talk about it, it's generally not in the context of our own lives, but of something we've read or seen in the theater or on TV, like the television series *13 Reasons Why*, based on a novel by the same title, which is about a young high school girl who dies by suicide. The hit Broadway musical *Dear Evan Hansen* also features a high school student suicide. Both are primarily about the feelings of family and friends left behind after the suicide, a rich subject to explore because such feelings are very complex. (An important note about this chapter: It is strictly about helping those in grief after a loved one dies by suicide. It is not about treating those who are having suicidal thoughts.)

If Only

When people grieve a death by suicide, they are inevitably haunted by their failure to have stopped it. Having talked to countless people who have lost a loved one to suicide, I can tell you that our minds can be very cruel. Our thoughts betray us and beat us up. One of the first things I say to such people is that when someone is intent on harming themselves, we may be powerless to prevent it. We should always try, but we cannot blame ourselves after the fact. Suicide is often an impulsive act, undertaken in a moment of despair. It can happen after years of psychotherapy, antidepressants, hospitalizations, and even shock therapy. Several recent celebrity deaths have driven that point home.

Still, our mind defaults to the *if-onlys*. My friend Vivian called me recently after her seventy-year-old father died by suicide. An untreated alcoholic, he had been threatening to do it for years, and it seemed inevitable that someday he would. But Vivian couldn't stop thinking, "If only I had gone to his house that day," "If only I'd made him see another doctor," "If only I'd intervened in his alcoholism." Such thoughts are a product of guilt, but they are also the mind's way of trying to assert control in an uncontrollable situation that has already happened.

Death by suicide is not a selfish act or even a choice. It's a sign of a mind that needs help. It's a horrific outcome to a tragic situation. We know from countless people who have survived a suicide attempt that they weren't looking to die. They felt they just couldn't continue to live in so much pain. Some suicides are driven by external circumstances—people are in overwhelming debt or they've lost the person they most loved or they have a serious chronic illness, or legal issues or substance-abuse problems. But many who died by suicide lived lives that can only be described as ideal, at least from the outside. They had families and friends who loved them, plenty of money, beautiful homes, professional success, yet they were tormented. Why? I think that for those of us without suicidal tendencies, it is almost impossible to imagine what it's like for those who do have them. Clinical depression itself is a serious illness, which can lead to suicide.

Although the latest studies from the Centers for Disease

Control and Prevention (CDC) reveal that suicide is a leading cause of death in the US, and suicide rates have increased
dramatically in the last few years, we still don't know enough
about it to really understand what causes it. Depression and
other mental health disorders certainly play a role, but suicide
is rarely caused by any single factor. Many people who die by
suicide are not known to have a diagnosed mental health condition at the time of death, although this simply may be because
there is such underreporting and misdiagnosis of mental illness.

Just as we know too little about what causes suicide, our
knowledge of how to prevent it is also limited. People say to
me, "No, no, you don't understand. I helped him once and I
should have been there to do it again," or "I actually could've
prevented it if only I'd known." I share the following reality
with them.

New hospitals are being built with mental health units
designed by specialized architects and firms. Among the most
crucial considerations in the construction of these facilities is
how to prevent death by suicide. Enormous amounts of thought
have gone into the design of everything from the doors and
even the door hinges to the bathroom fixtures, the lighting, the
cabinets and drawers, and the windows with shatter-resistant
glass. Once the hospitals are built, they are staffed by psychiatrists, psychiatric nurses, and technicians trained to prevent
death by suicide. And yet, despite all the care taken with design,
the specialized staffing, the inspections of all personal items, the
constant surveillance that deprives patients of their privacy, a
few people in these institutions will still die by suicide.

I gently tell those who are still feeling so much guilt, replaying their if-onlys, "Maybe you could've done something in that
moment, but if they were intent on ending their lives, if their
minds were in that much pain, you have to understand that
they would have found another moment when you weren't
there." They need to stop blaming themselves—and stop blaming the person who died.

The Stigma of Suicide

We don't understand the power of our words regarding suicide. The conventional way of recounting it is to say, "He/she committed suicide." The word "committed" is usually used in the context of crimes. A broken mind is a tragedy, not a crime. When we say it was "a successful suicide attempt," that seems to suggest that death by suicide can somehow be considered a success. When we say, "He was a suicide," we have made that person's cause of death his identity. I never heard anyone say, "She was a heart attack," or "He was an end-stage cancer." Jim is not a suicide. He is Jim who died by suicide.

Even if people are sympathetic, the stigma attached to suicide remains. It's difficult to speak about it in normal conversation or in mainstream discourse. You can go to a health center and easily get information about causes of cancer or disease, but not much about the causes of suicide.

People who lose a loved one to suicide often think that this doesn't happen in good families, or to good people. They may feel that suicide is a rare and shameful event and try to keep it quiet. But once they start to talk about what happened, they will almost certainly discover others who have gone through it, too, because it's actually the tenth most common cause of death in the United States. They may be shocked to find out how many of their acquaintances have had a death of someone dear to them through suicide.

Nonetheless, the stigma remains. Studies have shown that a family grieving after a death by suicide receives much less support than if their loved one died of cancer. Fewer people attend the funeral and the family receives fewer sympathy calls because of the false belief that the dead brought this upon themselves and therefore the death is not as worthy of being mourned. The family members themselves may feel this way, too. Since shame is part of the loss, some may invent a false story about the death, saying that their loved one died of a sudden heart attack or a stroke or whatever.

The condemnation of suicide is reinforced by most religions, which consider suicide to be a sin, although some of the more enlightened clergy are beginning to change their views on this. I made that point at one of my talks on death by suicide, and afterward a man approached me and said, "I hope what you are saying is true."

"Have you been touched by a death by suicide?" I asked him.

He teared up and said, "My mother was mentally ill. They diagnosed it as schizophrenia and she ended up dying by suicide. I was told by my priest that she would be denied entrance to heaven."

I looked at this poor man in his sixties who was in tears at the thought of his poor mother being locked out of heaven and destined to suffer forever. We would never think of blaming someone with stage IV cancer or picture them being kept out of heaven because of it. What about someone with stage IV bipolar disorder or stage IV schizophrenia? Does their disease deserve blame and exclusion? We begin to see how archaic our belief system is regarding mental illness.

Should we do more to prevent suicide? Absolutely. Should we work day and night to educate people about suicide? Yes. Should we raise awareness about mental illness and how it can cause our minds to turn in on ourselves? Without question, yes! In fact, if your loved one has died by suicide, this kind of work could be part of your search for meaning.

Routes to Freedom

Finding some kind of meaning in a death by suicide may seem impossible. The same feelings of hopelessness that caused a person to take their life may overwhelm the survivors. When I counsel people who have had a death by suicide, I tell them first that they have to separate the pain from the suffering. Pain is a natural reaction to death, whether it's by suicide or any other means, but suffering is what our mind does to us. Although this is something I often say to those who are grieving, it's particularly critical in these circumstances, because the mind often goes into overdrive to create hurtful, self-blaming stories about why the suicide occurred.

The path to freedom from the suffering caused by our minds is through finding meaning.

It's not an easy path. Death by suicide is often viewed as meaningless, but it need not be. People grieving such a death may find that meaning in their own time. One path many have taken is through involvement in organizations that help educate people about suicide. In fact, most suicide prevention organizations were founded by someone hoping to find some kind of meaning after a suicide.

A couple of years ago, I was speaking at a training session on death by suicide. One of the other speakers was documentary filmmaker Lisa Klein. Lisa shared with the group that her own interest in the subject was brought about because of the anguish she felt over the deaths of her father and brother. Both died by suicide within just a few months of each other, although the stigma was so great that the word was never spoken in her home. Lisa had come to talk to the group about *The S Word*, the documentary she directed about a suicide-attempt survivor turned suicide-awareness advocate who was on a mission to find fellow survivors and record their stories.

Lisa had already made a documentary about bipolar disorder, inspired by an older sister who had suffered from it all her life. After that she thought it was time to move on from the subject of mental disorders to less depressing material, until she realized there were more demons in her family to be dealt with. She said in an interview, "There is nothing depressing about working to prevent the kind of suffering that so many families have endured. The most depressing thing would be to remain silent and not do this movie." In searching for a way to make meaning out of the loss of her father and her brother, she ended up making a movie about suicide prevention, which introduced her to a thriving community of people who had attempted suicide and lived to help others. The stories they told about their struggles were filled with courage and insight as well as humor.

There are many paths to meaning, and if you search for them, you will eventually find them. In one of my groups, a woman named Joanne talked to us about her mother who had died by suicide more than a decade before. Joanne seemed so vulnerable; the sorrow that caused her to talk about it was so palpable, it was clear that the years that had passed had not taken away all the pain. "It isn't the easiest event to make meaning of," she said, "because our world isn't comfortable speaking about it. Over the last two years, I kept asking myself, 'What is this pain for? What else can I do with it? How can I create meaning?'

"My mom was raised in an era when people didn't talk about sexual assault or sexual abuse," she said. "But it happened to her and she was never able to recover from it. I still hesitate to talk about it because it's such a dark topic. My mother's father abused her at a time when there was little to no treatment for the trauma caused by being molested."

It's not surprising to find trauma in Joanne's mother's story. In many cases of death by suicide we find some mix of physical trauma, emotional trauma, mental illness, and addiction. For Joanne's mother the ramifications of her early abuse were lifelong.

My mother never stopped asking herself, "Why am I not lovable? Why did my father abuse me?" She was assaulted from age five to age twelve and her father threatened her with a gun if she told anyone. She was so traumatized by what had happened that she stopped speaking, and her father had her committed to a mental hospital. In those days they didn't know how to treat trauma. PTSD wasn't even a diagnosis yet.

After a few years of going in and out of the mental hospital, they treated her with extensive shock therapy and the doctors suggested she confront her father. When she did, his response was, "You're crazy. You have a brain fried from the shock treatment and you don't remember anything."

That made it worse for my mother. It was like the twisting of the knife.

Eventually my mother met my father at a restaurant where she was a hostess. I was born the year after they got married. As soon as she became a mother he began to see how stressed she was by her new responsibilities. He realized that she had serious mental problems to deal with. Luckily my father had a huge family that pitched in to help. Mom spent her life working as a hostess in various restaurants and as a greeter in a Walmart. She would often be told that she was so bright she could move up into management. But she had no desire to do that, and the only times she tried, it turned out badly. Once I asked her why she had always gravitated toward the kinds of jobs she took. She said she wanted people to feel welcome and wanted.

In later years my mother was diagnosed with schizophrenia and depression. The lack of resources for sexual assault victims and its impact on her life was devastating. After a while it became too much for her to bear. My mother took an overdose of a mixture of medications that ended her life. She left a suicide note that said, "I can't stand this anymore."

Joanne refused to let this be the end of the story. She needed and wanted to make some meaning out of her mother's tragic life. She accepted the fact that she could not help her mother, but she wanted to find a way to make her mother's suffering serve some good. She wanted to turn her pain into purpose. Eventually Joanne, who is a legal advocate, was able to use her professional skills to make a difference for other victims of sexual abuse. It took years, but the very public trial of a man accused of abuse caught her attention and spurred her to action.

"I watched what happened," she said, "when Jian Ghomeshi, a well-known Canadian musician and radio personality, went on trial on charges of sexually assaulting at least three women. He was found not guilty because the defense very skillfully focused on inconsistencies in details in the testimony of the women who claimed to have been assaulted, and on the fact that some of them had continued to have a relationship with him after the alleged assault (a behavior that happens in some abuse victims). The judge concluded from the case presented by the defense that the witnesses' accusations were 'tainted by outright deception.' But I knew that the kinds of inconsistencies the defense had been able to point out are typical of those who have undergone trauma and can't recollect details of the experience.

"Along with other advocates, we went on to change Canadian laws that would encourage education about sexual assault and trauma for judges. For me, being able to make some positive, vital contribution to how people in the legal system are educated about the kind of abuse that destroyed my mother's life diminished some of the pain I experienced and became my way of giving her a positive legacy."

I often ask those in grief if they could have one last communication with their loved ones, what would they say? This can be especially emotional for someone who is addressing a loved one who died by suicide, because grief often gets mixed up with guilt and anger. Perhaps because Joanna had found a way to make meaning out of what had happened to her mother, her feelings were not complicated. She was simply filled with love.

"I wouldn't want my mother to feel like she failed this life," Joanne said. "She had gigantic obstacles to face. In response to her last message, 'I can't stand it anymore,' I would tell her that I didn't blame her for the way she died. I would tell her that I love her unconditionally."

Children as young as seven have reported having suicidal thoughts. We do not realize how often young people die by suicide. Such deaths often occur after the end of a relationship, or because of bullying, trauma, or a variety of other factors. Young people are often very impulsive.

Jeff, a participant in one of my workshops for counselors, told me this story:

> When I was sixteen and a sophomore in high school, I was friendly with a fourteen-year-old eighth-grader, Tim, who took his own life. He was a neighborhood kid. I'd known him ever since I was in kindergarten when I attended a half-day program in the morning and then, because both of my parents worked, I went to Tim's house in the afternoon, where his mother took care of me for the rest of the day.
>
> Tim and I were always friendly, and we'd say hi in the hallways, but because of our age difference, which is a big deal when you're that young, I didn't really know him well. When he died, that was my first real experience with a peer who had died by suicide. I remember how his death rocked our school. He'd been very popular, and he always seemed like a happy kid. He wasn't captain of the football team or anything like that, but he was always smiling, personable, and friendly. Everybody was shocked because his death seemed to come out of nowhere.
>
> I remember wondering if any of my friends were as unhappy as he was, but weren't showing it, just like him. I tried to make sure to talk to my friends a little more, to draw them out a bit. "Hey, are you doing okay?" I'd ask. I wanted to make sure that anybody who was really sad would feel they could talk to me about what was going on.
>
> Right out of high school, I started volunteering with a youth ministry program at my church. I got my social work license, and I've been practicing counseling ever since. I've used Tim's story in my work to try to help kids who seem like they might be troubled, especially the silent sufferers who think they can't tell anyone what's going on with them. I make sure that kids who need help are getting it. I offer them a safe place to talk about themselves. I try to ask questions, to listen well, and to help them through their difficult circumstances.

I keep a picture of Tim in my office in a desk drawer. Sometimes I show it to my clients as a way of saying, "This young man was a friend of mine who suffered a lot and took his own life." I want them to know that I'm familiar with kids who have problems like theirs, and that I don't judge them for having suicidal thoughts. I tell them, "I want to make sure you're going to be okay. I went into this field to help kids like you, so you wouldn't have to suffer quietly."

I've also done a lot of counseling with teens who have had someone they love die by suicide. I try to help them put the pieces back together. Several years ago, I worked with a young man whose best friend had died by suicide. They were in middle school, the same age, and the death had occurred three years earlier. He was still very depressed. I showed him Tim's picture and told him a little bit about my story and how I dealt with the loss. I could sense it was an important moment, because he said he felt like he was talking to someone who really understood what he was going through. That seemed to be the turning point in his healing.

A few years ago, I sent Tim's mother (my babysitter when I was in kindergarten) a message on Facebook. I'd been debating it for years, and I finally wrote, "Hey, I just want to share a little piece of my story without causing you any undue suffering. Some wounds never fully heal, so I've dedicated my professional life to helping kids like Tim find some help and hopefully get better."

Jeff said she called him right away. "I'm really glad you messaged me," she told him. "I still miss Tim. His loss is something I've been wrestling with for years." She cried for a few minutes and Jeff listened on the phone. "It's comforting to know that Tim's death has given you purpose," she said, "and you've helped other kids in similar situations."

Jeff did two things that helped Tim's mother. First, he witnessed her grief. Even all these years later, it was important for her to know that the life and death of her son still mattered in the world. Second, he shared how he had made meaning of the loss, which brought her meaning, too.

Most of us find it very hard to understand what was going on in the minds of those who died by suicide—probably because we look at life through minds that are healthy and not suffering from depression or other mental issues. I have a suicide note I've kept for many years, which I think gives a lot of insight into the kind of pain that might lead someone to suicide. When someone who is grieving says, "I just don't get it," this letter helps them understand.

Dear Mom, Dad, and Gregory,

If I am successful and can go through with it this time, I want you to know I am really sorry, but I have no more hope for myself. I feel so stuck in the deepest of ruts. I want to free myself from all this misery I've put upon myself. I have forever lost myself, my soul, and my purpose in life. I don't know what is right anymore.

I am worn out from thinking so negatively and being unable to free myself from this torture. I feel so much fear around others. I've thought of lots of ways to kill myself, yet always think about you guys, Mom, Dad, and Gregory, and have really been fighting it with everything I have. Sometimes I think there is hope for me, but then I start doubting myself. I know this seems like the weakest of things to do and it probably is. Yet I really feel damaged, and it's nobody's fault but mine. I am so sorry for all that I am putting you all through, something that is so unfair and not really respectable, but I am weak, and I don't think I'd make it. I'm hoping if I go through with this, God will understand. The worst loss to me is you guys, my family, and yet I don't know any other way to make it better. I feel so sick for all, but I can't change this feeling inside my head. I am so sorry, Mom. I love all of you. It's just time for me to rise above this planet and free my soul from the torture I'm putting on it and have put upon you. I wish I could describe what I feel inside . . .

the anger, the pain, and my inability to connect with it or to make it better.

Love is all I wanted. At least this is what I feel like now, and I don't have love within anymore. I have terror of myself as not being the loving person that I am. It's not me. I don't even know me anymore. I tried, and this is nobody's fault but my own. Yet if I could show you how much I love all of you, I promise I will, just not in this matter. I will do it in spirit. I hope God looks after me, and I hope he understands and forgives me. I am going to miss you so much that I want to stay and work out these problems. I can't do this. I can't stop the flow of energy, but God is just no help anymore. I feel stuck. I'm so upset that I have not done anything in life. I feel totally academically incapable. I am sorry, and I love all of you. Please forgive me. It was not any of you. It is all me.

Love,
Robert

Robert went through with the suicide that time, and his letter illustrates so many kinds of pain that caused him to do so. He had a glimpse of the person he wanted to be, but he couldn't get there. We see his struggle and his sense of failure, his disappointment that life was not going the way he wanted. The absence of hope is like a thread running through the entire letter, as is his guilt over what he was doing to the people he loved so much. Robert battled more demons in one day than many of us battle in a year. All he wanted was to end his suffering. For those he left behind, however, he left a clear message that it wasn't their fault. His words helped them understand that pain was the cause of his death, not anything they did or did not do.

And now, because his parents have so generously allowed his letter to be shared, his words are helping other people who are grieving a death by suicide, letting them understand that they are not to blame. In that way, he left a gift that enabled his parents to make something meaningful from their loss.

Meaning can arrive through the most unlikely of routes. Wanda told me the following story, which began with the illness of her cat, Samantha, who was diagnosed with cancer of the nasal cavity.

We saw a specialist at a veterinarian teaching hospital, and Samantha did well for a while, but her cancer was aggressive, and it spread. Usually when I took her to the clinic I went with my husband, but when I went for what turned out to be the last time, I was alone, and it was decided that the best thing for Samantha was to be euthanized, which was heartbreaking.

I was deeply moved by the amount of time the veterinarian, Dr. Christine, took with me, both before the euthanasia, when she helped me make that very difficult decision, and after. Her kindness helped me a great deal. But I was taken aback by how much I grieved Samantha's death in the months that followed. One thing that comforted me was thinking about the kindness of the veterinarian, so after receiving my master's in social work, I decided to get a veterinarian certificate to support our animal companions and those who take care of them.

Two years later I wanted to tell Dr. Christine, who had been so loving, kind, and tender, how much she had inspired me. But when I dropped by the office to see her, the people behind the desk told me she no longer worked there.

"Where is she?" I asked. "I want to get in touch with her."

They said they had no further information to give out, but something felt strange about their response. I told them the story about how she had inspired me, and they began tearing up. Finally, someone said, "We don't often tell people, but Dr. Christine died by suicide about a year ago." I was shocked, but they told me it was not unusual for veterinarians to die this way.

I did some research and discovered that of ten thousand actively practicing American veterinarians, one in six—14.4 percent of males and 19.1 percent of females—have considered suicide, which is three times the US national average, and similar to the suicide rate among medical doctors, too. For both vets and medical doctors, it can be very hard for them to see their patients suffer and die.

I decided I needed to do something to help, so I facilitated a support group for local veterinarians. I try to drop by their offices and chat for a minute, encouraging them to connect with other veterinarians instead of isolating themselves. I remind them how important their work is. That's my meaning and my gift to Dr. Christine.

Here's the hard truth: people who die by suicide don't die because of anything we did or didn't do. They died because they were mentally compromised, and their suffering mind told them that was the only way to escape excruciating pain.

We can live our life in a way that honors them and brings hope to their struggle. All life has meaning, no matter how it comes to an end.

CHAPTER EIGHT

Complicated Relationships

Be kind, for everyone is fighting a battle you know nothing about.

—Anonymous

In grief, you want to feel that your closest friends and family members are sensitive to your feelings, that they understand your sadness. Many do. And then there are the people who always seem to disappoint. You can rail against them as you have every right to do, or you can simply accept them for who they are. That's a choice you have to make, and in my opinion, either is valid. However, hoping they will be different than they are only leads to more turmoil.

When I hear stories about the inappropriate, tactless things people say or do to those who are grieving, I always ask, "Is this the first time they acted like that?" The answer is usually no. People tend to be consistent. The narcissistic mother continues to think your loss is all about her. The competitive friend thinks he has suffered a bigger loss. The controlling sibling tells you how to fix things. Part of our work in these complicated relationships is to see the people as themselves, and to decide, from a place of calm and detachment, how to respond to them.

Zoey, a woman I worked with, told me that her friend said the stupidest thing to her when she was grieving over her sister's death. Now they were no longer talking.

"What did she say?" I asked.

"When my sister died, she said, 'Well, at least you won't be in her shadow anymore.'"

It sounded like such an out-of-the-blue comment that I had to wonder what might have preceded it. I asked, "Had you two ever talked about you feeling that you were living in your sister's shadow?"

"Well, yes, that was an ongoing issue with my sister."

"Did your friend ever say anything stupid before?"

"Yes, stupid stuff rolls out of her mouth all the time."

"Did you expect that stupid stuff would stop rolling out of her mouth just because someone died?"

"Well, yes. When someone dies . . . "

"We all become evolved instantly? Right?"

She laughed and so did I. She got the point. People are who they are, and they don't change just because we need them to. If they are important enough to us, we will overlook their insensitivity. If they're not, we may consider letting the friendship go.

Of course, some relationships are not chosen, such as those we have with our children. When they disappoint us at times when we most want to see them rise to the occasion, we need to try to understand what is going on with them. I worked with a couple whose younger daughter had died in a rafting accident. Their older daughter, Brooke, was a teenager. Her mother described her as moody, her father described her as downright rebellious. At the funeral home when they were making final arrangements, Brooke said she needed to go to the bathroom. After thirty minutes her dad went to check on her and found her outside on the phone, talking to one of her friends, smoking. He was furious. Three nights after the funeral she sneaked out to meet friends and lied about it the next morning. The deceptions and lies continued over the following weeks, and her parents were shocked by her behavior. They couldn't believe she seemed so unaffected by her sister's death and so indifferent to their feelings.

Two months after the death of their daughter, I met the parents at a support group, where they talked about how upset they were by Brooke's behavior. I asked if this behavior was consistent with the way she had acted before her sister's death. The answer was yes, but they expected that what they had been through as a family would have brought them closer together and helped her to be kinder.

"You hoped that this death was going to turn your family into a tender Hallmark card kind of family," I said. "This is a common fantasy. We often mistakenly think that a death will be a catalyst for personal growth, that it will improve our character and create a sense of unity and solidarity. And it's true that death does sometimes bring about a new maturity. But many times, the emotional upheaval it causes just magnifies our immaturity, and this is particularly likely to be the case with a teenager. Teenagers and some adults don't know how to manage their feelings, and in an instance like this one, they probably have very complicated feelings of their own. Maybe Brooke doesn't know how to express her grief or she only knows how to express it with anger. Maybe she and her sister had a contentious relationship and now she's feeling guilty. Maybe she doesn't want her friends to know how much she's hurting. She doesn't want anything to change and just wants to do normal defiant teenage things. Or she resents all the focus on her sister and is feeling that her parents aren't paying attention to her. Maybe she thinks that having good times with her friends will make her feel better and a million other possibilities. Loss is a strong current that infuses everything it touches. We hope for more love and compassion. But that same current also runs through resentment, entitlement, and oppositional behavior. We grieve in character, both good and bad!"

Finishing Our Unfinished Business

It would be nice if all our relationships could be wrapped up in a bow with all our lifetime issues resolved before death comes. Unfortunately, that is not how real life works. Elisabeth Kübler-

Ross talked about this as our "unfinished business." After the death of a loved one, we are often left with unfinished business—complications that leave us with anger and guilt, regret and recriminations. Our feelings may stem from something as recent as yesterday's argument, or as old as something going back to childhood. The relationship simply could be strained, or there could be a longtime or permanent estrangement.

There is of course no way of bringing a resolution to a relationship after a death. The unfinished business will remain unfinished. But what if we know that someone with whom we have one of these complicated relationships is dying? This presents us with both a dilemma and an opportunity. Do we want to be there for that person, despite the issues that divided us in the past? Or do we want to keep our distance? And if we do show up, will we even be welcome?

I know two sisters who had one of those difficult relationships, dating back to their childhood. Rochelle was the one who got good grades and followed all the rules, while her sister, Lisa, did poorly in school, rebelled against her parents, and was often in trouble. Rochelle and Lisa fought constantly, and Rochelle resented her sister for making family life so difficult. As teenagers, Rochelle washed the car and Lisa took it out without permission and wrecked it. They were like oil and water with each other, never mixing, always fighting.

Rochelle went to college, then medical school, where she met her husband, and the two of them became doctors and had three children. They bought a house not far from her parents and she was very involved with family, as well as active in the local community. Lisa, on the other hand, did not go to college. She had always wanted to be an actress and moved to New York City with dreams of being on Broadway. Like many other young women who want to go on the stage, she supported herself by waitressing, but once when she lost a waitress job, she asked her parents if she could borrow money from them. When Rochelle heard about that, she told her parents they should cut Lisa off so she could finally grow up.

By the time the two women hit their thirties, Rochelle had become a successful doctor, and Lisa, who was now getting small parts on Broadway, seemed finally to be finding her footing as an actress. The fact that they had both found what they wanted in life didn't seem to help matters between them, however. When they gathered at their parents' house for Christmas or Thanksgiving, Rochelle thought Lisa was self-centered, and Lisa thought Rochelle was rigid and uptight. They tried to keep the peace during these family events, but the tension was always there.

Lisa eventually got a lead role in a Broadway show and her career really started to take off. At about the same time, Rochelle found out she had brain cancer. She took chemo but knew her time was limited. After Rochelle's diagnosis, Lisa came home to spend some time with her. One day, Lisa said, "I hope you get better soon. Your kids need a mom. Your patients love you as their doctor. Maybe at some point you will be strong enough to come see my show."

Rochelle snapped, "It's always about you, isn't it?"

Lisa was terribly hurt by the comment. She had been to Rochelle's college graduation, medical school graduation, and attended the grand opening of her office. She'd also celebrated Rochelle's children's birthdays with her. Lisa felt that she finally had something good in her life and she wanted to share it with her sister, but Rochelle wasn't interested. Nonetheless, when Lisa's show ended, she came home to help Rochelle, whose health had dramatically declined. Lisa was there every day to help with the kids and take Rochelle to doctors' appointments.

When Rochelle asked Lisa why she was doing this, she said, "Because you're my sister." Rochelle died eight months later. A few months after the death, one of Lisa's cousins visited her in New York. She told Lisa that, having watched them grow up, she had always been aware of how difficult their relationship was. She was curious about what had made it so hard for them to get along. "I never wanted Rochelle to be any different than she was," Lisa told her cousin, "but she always wanted me to be different. I came across as bad to her, but I was just creative."

The cousin was surprised and impressed that after all the bad blood between them, Lisa had gone home to care for her sister. "How did you find it in yourself to help her so much?"

"I just played my part," Lisa said. "I learned in acting and in my life that my job reflects my character. My job is how I respond to situations and other people. How people choose to play their characters is not for me to evaluate. My one and only job is my own character. I showed up for her, just like I wanted to."

Lisa discovered that at the end of the day, in our most complex and often frustrating relationships, we can only be responsible for our side of the street. How Rochelle behaved was not something she could control or judge. How she herself behaved was completely within her control, and she chose the path that seemed right for her.

I believe Lisa's decision came from a place of great wisdom. Too often when we deal with people in complicated relationships, we focus on their reactions. If I do this for them, will they appreciate it? Will it be reciprocated? Or will they reject me in some hurtful fashion? I always encourage people to do kind things with no expectations. Expectations are resentments under construction.

Each of us has to make our own choices about how to deal with complicated relationships, and the more complex they are, the harder the choice. The choice becomes even harder when death approaches. Or maybe it's easier sometimes, because it's so clarifying. I think that may have been the case for Trisha, who had been estranged from her mother for many years.

Trisha, a special education teacher, had a tough upbringing with a mentally ill mother. Her mother wanted to take care of her, but because of her illness she couldn't. Looking back, Trisha reflected, "Today my mother would be considered bipolar, but then no one knew what was wrong. It started when I was about six years old. She went through these periods where she hated me, and she wouldn't buy me any clothes even though she was buying clothes for my brother. I was so neglected and unkempt that once, when a family member came to visit, she took me shopping and paid for me to have a haircut. My mother wasn't just neglectful. She was physically abusive to me for no reason. As a child you don't understand that your mom is mentally ill. You think that if you're treated this way, it must be because you did something wrong."

I asked her how she had coped with that as a child.

"Not well," she said. "It's no surprise that I started drinking and smoking pot at thirteen years old. I wanted to be numb. I was lucky I didn't get into more trouble during those teenage years. I finally left home for good when I was twenty-two and I never returned, except for brief visits."

"Did your mother resent you for leaving?"

"She did, and I felt tormented about that, but my mother was so destructive to me that I decided I could only have a meaningful life if I minimized my contact with her. For a while I went to see her once a year, until one time when she slammed the door in my face and refused to let me in. I called her later and she screamed how much she hated me. After that I chose not to have my mother in my life. People judged me for not going to see her, but they had no idea what I had gone through. I cut off all contact with her at that point."

"No contact at all?" I asked her.

"I sent her a Christmas card every year. Because I wanted to. I did it for me."

Like Lisa, she took responsibility for her own behavior. How her mother responded or didn't had no impact on what she did.

Trisha continued. "During the time we were estranged, family members told me that my mother was hospitalized after attempting to harm herself. She was in a coma when she was found, and when she came out of it, she turned to God. I think she found meaning in that, and her church was accepting of her. But I had no interest in resuming our relationship. It had been too painful.

"I hadn't spoken with her for over twenty years when I found out that my mother had an aggressive cancer. I lived in Massachusetts and I was teaching summer school. After much consideration, I decided to take time off to go to Wisconsin where my mother lived to be with her at the end. When I arrived, the cancer had spread everywhere, and it had gone to her brain. During that week I spent with her, there was no discussion as to why we hadn't spoken all those years. I was with my mother every day. She died a week later around 7:00 a.m. with no one in the room but me. I was holding her hand and rubbing her head."

"How was that for you?" I asked.

"It gave me some peace. She was leaving, and it was meaningful to me to be with her at the end. I was fine with the decision not to speak with her for those twenty years, but I felt love in the moment of her passing. Although she was mentally ill, she had played the role of mother as best she could. By the time she died, I had gained the maturity I needed to understand that she didn't choose to be bipolar, and the way she treated me wasn't about me but about her illness."

Forgiveness

Forgiveness can be a difficult area for all of us. We build up blocks that bind us for many years. It can be very tricky to deal with in grief. First of all, not all can be forgiven. There are just some dragons we can't slay in this lifetime.

Forgiveness is a wonderful gift for those in grief who are consumed by unhappiness and resentment toward another person.

There have been many models and types of forgiveness. I usually discuss these three possibilities:

1. Indirect forgiveness: you do it all inside yourself.
2. Direct forgiveness: the other person comes to you for forgiveness and you forgive them. The problem is that they rarely come to you.
3. Conditional forgiveness: the other person asks for forgive-

ness and you may or may not give it, depending on many factors. Did you think they were sincere? Was it timely? Do they understand the pain they caused?

Of these three, I find that indirect forgiveness is the one that works most often. No one else is needed, living or dead.

We can learn to forgive ourselves and those who have hurt us by not letting someone's actions define us. Even though forgiveness after murder is rare, it does come up. I was working with a woman who was consumed with the murder of her sister a decade earlier. It had destroyed her life. The murderer was locked up for the rest of his life, but she was in prison also. She was looking for a way out of her pain, and I asked her about the possibility of forgiving him. She responded with "Never! There's no way."

I explained that forgiveness was not about condoning what he had done.

"I could never, I hate that word," she said.

Some have a negative history with the word "forgiveness." If that is the case, I might substitute the words "letting go."

I told her, "It's a tragedy that he took two lives."

"No. It was only my sister."

"Yes," I said, "but he took your life, too. What if you're not giving him a pardon but letting go of him? He doesn't deserve a place in your soul or psyche. He lives there all the time without contributing or paying any rent. He doesn't deserve the space."

"I never thought about it like that," she said.

"What if the word 'forgiveness' also means disconnection?" I said. "What if forgiveness was about disconnecting from his murderous actions? You deserve to be free without giving him another moment of your life."

She sat silently for a long time. Then she said with a new strength, "That changes everything."

Forgiveness opens our hearts when we are stuck in the prison of resentment. We get to be right, but we never get to be happy.

When we're talking about lesser infractions by our family and friends, you may disagree and say, "But you don't know what *they* did to me; it's unforgivable." If you are unwilling to forgive, it can be a terrible thing to do to yourself. Bitterness is like swallowing a teaspoon of poison every day. It accumulates and harms you. It's impossible to be healthy and free when you keep yourself bound to the past.

I use four ways to forgive.

1. I picture the person as an infant. There were born innocent.
2. I think of them growing up and someone wounding them. Wounded people wound people. They wound you because that is how they have been taught.
3. You can forgive the person, but not the action. Maybe the stupid thing they said at the funeral does feel unforgivable. But you have had twenty years of friendship.
4. I remember I'm not perfect, either.

I often use the last one. A friend of mine suggested me for a keynote lecture for her national organization. At dinner the night before when I asked how she was, she said, "It's been rough." She had been battling cancer.

I said, "I think I heard that you were dealing with that."

She said, "Yes, David, I called you and told you and you said you would call me back and you never did."

I knew she was telling the truth and I can imagine how it happened. I answered the phone and heard it was cancer, but perhaps I was in airport security or an inappropriate place for that type of call. I said I'd call back, time passed, more calls and emails came in, and I got lost.

I deeply apologized for my actions. I'm not someone who forgets to call people back when they have cancer, but that is what I did. When I recognize I'm human and I make mistakes, I can forgive others for their mistakes.

One of the biggest spiritual lessons we can learn is to understand that everyone is doing the best they can at any given moment. No one looks in the mirror in the morning and says, "I think I'll be a real jerk today."

People can only do so much with the understanding, awareness, and knowledge they have. This is not to say that their behavior is acceptable or excusable. The incident you are holding on to is over. Perhaps it's long over. It will help to remember that forgiveness is seldom for "them." It is for *you*.

Even if it is for you, you must want it, and not everyone does. Kim Goldman is unfortunately known for the murder of her brother, Ron Goldman, by O. J. Simpson. The killer was acquitted in the criminal trial and later found guilty in the civil trial. He went on to write a book called *If I Did It*.

I sat down with Kim to talk about the horrific and very public loss of her brother. For all she has been through, she is a strong, happy, articulate woman with a sweet, tender heart. We talked about the concept of forgiveness. Kim, like many people who have had a family member murdered, felt the trendy pressure to forgive. Kim is being asked to forgive someone who has no remorse.

When people know that I have spent time with her and talked to her about her grief, they will tell me, "She should forgive and just move on."

I will often ask, "Is that what helped you after your loved one was murdered?"

They will say, "No, my loved one wasn't murdered."

"How did they die?" I'll ask.

All too often I get a quick, "Oh, I haven't had a death, I just believe in forgiveness."

I tell them I do too, but it's easier said than done. Outsiders who have not walked a mile in her shoes or felt the brutality of murder can easily say, "But she will be happy again and finally get over it."

Kim is happy, she has a wonderful family, she still misses her brother and sees no value in forgiving. She said, "I'm not looking for it or working on it, and I'm not offering forgiveness."

Ironically, she receives lots of hate mail telling her that she should forgive.

Stakes Are Higher in Grief

When you've had a complicated relationship and the person suddenly dies, you no longer have the opportunity to sort out the problems that kept you apart, or to express your love. This can make the grieving process particularly difficult. A woman, Sally, told me a story about her brother with whom she had a loving but often argumentative relationship. As children, they had often fought, and as adults, they sometimes ignored each other's phone calls for several days after an argument. One day they had one of their usual disagreements, and for three days Sally didn't return any of his calls. It was just another disagreement, not much different from the others, and she knew that pretty soon they'd be making up as they always did. The next call she received, however, was not from him, but from someone else telling her that her brother had had a heart attack and died. All of a sudden, ignoring his calls for three days became the worst thing she had ever done in her life. And somewhere in her mind there was the idea that her anger with him had caused his death.

We all have a tendency to indulge in this kind of magical thinking—the belief that our thoughts and feelings can have an effect on the outside world. But when I asked Sally to think this through rationally, to consider that they'd had lots of fights before, and none of them had killed her brother, she of course realized that nothing she had done had caused him to have a heart attack. That didn't take away her regret that their last words to each other had been unpleasant ones. As we spoke, however, and I asked about her other memories of their relationship, she told me many stories about how close they were and what a good time they had together. After her divorce was final, her brother had invited her to join them on a family cruise. "I felt lost and he knew the cruise would be a good pattern breaker." Her memories helped her to put that last fight into context, to see it as just one episode in a long, complicated, but ultimately very loving relationship.

I recently heard from a woman, Carol, who spoke about the last day she spent with her teenage daughter. Because her washing machine was broken, Carol went to a laundromat and took her daughter with her. Being a typical teenager, the girl complained bitterly about having to waste part of her weekend helping her mother do laundry. Carol had grown up in very modest circumstances, without a washer and dryer, so she had spent plenty of time at laundromats during her own teenage years. She felt her daughter was acting entitled, which offended her, and she lost patience with her complaints.

She yelled at her, "Do you think I want to be here at the laundromat? Do you think this is my idea of having fun? Could you act any more spoiled?"

Carol could have ignored her. She could have waited until they were no longer in a public place to tell her how inappropriate she thought her behavior was. Instead, she blew up. And her daughter blew up, too.

"That's it. I'm out of here," her daughter said, and she ran out the door. For most people, this sounds like normal teenage drama that would typically end with the girl slinking home later and her mother doling out the appropriate punishment. But that's not how Carol's story ended. When her daughter left, she met up with some friends who had borrowed a car and was killed in a car crash.

Afterward, Carol tormented herself. "Why couldn't I have ignored her behavior? Why didn't I realize that teenagers can be this way sometimes? Why did I humiliate her in public? If I hadn't lost my temper, she'd still be alive."

Both of these stories illustrate the guilt people feel when death intervenes before a relationship can be mended. These complicated relationships often carry blame, and I ask grievers to consider Occam's razor, a scientific and philosophic rule commonly described as "the simplest answer is most often correct." Too many what-ifs are a sign that we're veering away from the truth of the situation. Part of my work is helping people understand the simple true reasons, not the complex ones, that are born of the what-ifs. Not answering the phone doesn't cause death, heart attacks do—that's the simple truth. Once they realize they didn't cause the death, they still may have guilt to untangle from the relationship. I suggest two different methods for dealing with guilt in these situations.

I ask the person to close their eyes and picture their loved one at a healthier, happier time. I ask them to think of a moment their loved one was kind. Sally might say to her brother, "I'm sorry I didn't take your call. I love you and I never meant to hurt you or ignore you." I might ask Carol to say to her daughter, "I'm so sorry I blew up at the laundromat. I love you and I never meant to embarrass you." I believe if you say you are sincerely sorry from your heart, your loved one will still feel it in theirs.

The other option for untangling that guilt is to make a "living amends." This is where you take the action you wish would have occurred and do it with others for the rest of your life.

Below you will find a sample of language you could use to set an intention for a living amends, using your own words.

My living amends to my [mother, brother, husband, etc.] is I will or will not [the intended action]. That will be my amends, my living, breathing apology.

For example, I might have Sally say, "My living amends to my brother is that after an argument with anyone else, I will take their calls. That will be my amends, my living, breathing apology." Perhaps Carol could say, "My living amends to my daughter is that I won't blow up publicly at anyone else. That will be my amends, my living, breathing apology." If you never told your loved one who died that you loved them, then you might say, "My living amends to my loved one is whenever I love someone, I'll tell them. That will be my amends, my living, breathing apology." Once we deal with guilt and make living amends, we can begin to fully grieve the person who died.

Obituaries and Eulogies: Truth in Packaging

In our modern world we are losing touch with important rituals. But this is our last public chance to say goodbye to the complicated relationships in our lives. We tend to idealize those who have died, such as the friend who struggled to write a glowing, loving eulogy for her mother, who was by no means a glowing, lovely person. I have often seen a member of the clergy presiding over a funeral for a person he or she didn't know. When Frank died, his widow said afterward that it was a beautiful service. Too bad it had nothing to do with Frank, she added. The funerals that are most memorable and touching are the ones that describe the person in full—the good parts and at least some of the bad. Often a person's character flaws—stubbornness, willfulness, arrogance, flamboyance, a determination to shock, rebelliousness, rule breaking, etc.—are also part of what made that person special and unique. The best eulogies will always take into account all the facets of the person's character, rather than try to make him into some kind of bland angel.

The same is true when we are writing an obituary. Another friend of mine whom I've known for thirty-five years always described her father as a monster. Given the stories she told about him, it was clear she had plenty of supporting evidence for that description, but she never cut off contact with him. She saw him regularly and was with him when he died. Afterward she wrote an amazing obit that managed to pay tribute to him by describing the extremely colorful and adventurous life he had lived. She also hinted at the fact that he'd been a very difficult man—something to the effect that he was one of a kind, as indeed he was. That authenticity resonates in our grief.

It witnesses the person, the complications, and the realities of the relationship. The act of writing the obituary allowed her to review and celebrate the many aspects of his life without obfuscating the dark side.

I remember seeing families gathered around a desk, trying to bang out an obituary that captured the essence of their loved ones. Should we say that he could never remember the end of a joke? Or mention that children drove him crazy and he was so glad he never had any of his own? Should we say that she kept a list and you were on it or off it, depending on your recent actions?

Obits can be as memorable as the person was, especially when they capture our uniqueness. Take actress Iva Withers's obituary in *The New York Times*, for example: "If there were a Tony Award for best understudy, Iva Withers might well have won repeatedly during her nearly three decades on Broadway. Though she appeared in the first Broadway run of musicals like *Carousel, Oklahoma!* and *Guys and Dolls*, she never originated a starring role of her own."

The obit continues to describe how Withers became the first actress to play the lead in two hit shows in one day. She played *Carousel* in the afternoon and *Oklahoma!* that night without a problem.

Humor can be a sweet reminder of who the person was in life and death. One of my favorites obits is about a man, Scott, who was described as a "fun-loving, kind, and caring man." It's easy to see why his family included a little bit of humor when writing his obituary.

The obituary explains that Scott was a lifelong football fan. He loved the Cleveland Browns and he "respectfully requested six Cleveland Browns pallbearers so the Browns could let him down one last time." The obituary closes by instructing friends and family to wear Cleveland Browns clothing to the service in his honor.

Luckily, obits still appear in newspapers and online, but all too often these days they are replaced by a social media post, a short announcement followed by a long list of "sorry for your loss" comments that exclude the wholeness of the person.

One woman shared that after she had witnessed her friend's social media post of photos and elaborate descriptions of endless meals that her friend had eaten, writing the comment "sorry for your loss" seemed inadequate and inauthentic. When responding to loss, we will never be able to reflect the magnitude of all that death has taken from us. With that in mind, we must show respect with more than platitudes.

CHAPTER NINE

Child Loss

A wife who loses a husband is called a widow. A husband who loses a wife is called a widower. A child who loses his parents is called an orphan. There is no word for a parent who loses a child. Lose your child and you're . . . nothing.

—Tennessee Williams

Barbara Bush, who was married to one US president and the mother of another, said that she didn't fear death. That might be because she faced it earlier in her life in the most heartbreaking way. In 1953, soon after she and her husband, George H. W. Bush, moved to Midland, Texas, their three-year-old daughter complained about feeling tired. This was worrisome, because Pauline Robinson "Robin" Bush, the much-doted-upon only girl of the Bush kids, was usually as rowdy as her older brother, George W., and her baby brother, Jeb. Barbara took her to a pediatrician, who decided to do some tests on her.

When the doctor called the Bushes a few days later, his diagnosis was shockingly abrupt. Robin had leukemia. Bush wrote in her 1994 memoir that the doctor's advice was, "Tell no one, go home, forget that Robin is sick, make her comfortable, and love her. This will happen very quickly." Seven months later, Robin died with her parents in the room. For one last time, Barbara combed her little girl's hair and held her.

The Bushes buried their daughter in a family plot in Greenwich, Connecticut, and in 2000, they moved her remains to a burial plot on the grounds of the George H. W. Bush Library in Texas, where the former president and first lady are now buried, too. For sixty-five years, Robin remained front and center in Mrs. Bush's conversation. When the first lady was on her deathbed, she said she was looking forward to being with Robin once again. Barbara left behind five children who loved her dearly, fourteen grandchildren, seven great-grandchildren, and a husband of more than seventy-three years—but the daughter she lost was never far from her mind.

A child's death is one of the most challenging experiences anyone can live through. After my son David died, I thought about all the grieving parents I'd counseled. Their excruciating losses had brought tears to my eyes and I had had great admiration for the courage they found to keep going after such a devastating loss. I had sat with them in that pain and heard it described so often I thought I really understood it. But when I felt the pain of my own son's death, I wanted to write a note to each and every one of those clients saying, "I'm so sorry, I had no idea how much this hurts."

My friend Ann told me the story of the death of her son, Jim. Twenty years old, he came home from college for the Christmas holidays and got sick on the day he was scheduled to return to school.

I was at the hospital where I worked, and when I got home, Jim was complaining of a bad headache. I asked him to say a little bit more about his headache, but he just kept repeating that it was really bad. I gave him a pain reliever and watched for signs that he was getting worse. I thought he had caught my husband's cold.

Later that night Jim was watching a football game in his room, and when he got out of bed, I could hear him vomiting in the bathroom. I went to check on him and saw that he was having strokelike symptoms, so I called 911 and they whisked him away to the hospital. Jim started to lose consciousness on the way, and by the time we got to the hospital, they had to

would always ask the paramedics, "Were they wearing their seat belts?" I believe that on a subconscious level there was the sense that if they weren't wearing their seat belts, they were to blame for their deaths, but if we wear ours, we will be able to keep ourselves safe. Death can't strike us at random. But unfortunately, it does.

In my grief work, I've been called in on many horrific disasters, and those who lost loved ones often want to know the cause, or whom to blame. When we provide disaster counseling, we often use the *Titanic* as an example. There wasn't a single factor that sank the ship; it was a chain of events. The ship was trying to set a speed record for crossing the Atlantic. If it had been going slower, there might have been enough time to save it. Binoculars that should have been available in the pilothouse were missing. If they had been in place, the crew might have been able to spot the unusually large number of icebergs, caused by unseasonable weather. If there had been fewer icebergs, the ship might not have crashed into one of them. If the cargo areas had had ceilings, the inflow of water could have been contained. And on top of all that, if there had been enough lifeboats, many more people could have been saved. If any one of these factors had been different, maybe *everyone* could have been saved.

The question of blame—very often self-blame—comes up with particular urgency when a child has died. Parents feel responsible for everything that happens to their children. Any grieving parent is likely to have haunting, guilt-ridden, late-night thoughts that boil down to, "If I had been a better parent, my child would still be alive." The truth is that 99 percent of them were wonderful parents. Still, they feel like they didn't do enough. They think they should have recognized the symptoms quicker or taken their child to the doctor sooner or found the miracle drug that would cure the disease. If their child died by suicide or because of a drug addiction problem, they probably did do everything they could—therapy, counseling, rehab, maybe even hospitalizations—over the years to try to deal with what was troubling their child, but still they think they should have done more.

It's hard for us to accept that early deaths just happen. But despite our best efforts, they do. The most stellar parents have children who die young and it isn't anyone's fault. But because we are so accustomed to taking responsibility for everything that happens to our children, we can't help but wonder what we could have done differently to change the outcome. There will never be a satisfying answer to this question.

If your child has died, you can honor your child's life in time, at your own pace, by not allowing the loss to consume you. Instead of withdrawing from the world in bitterness and grief, you can use all that love to reengage with your partner, your other children, and your family members and friends. Then look into your heart to see how you can find meaning from your loss. Many grieving parents have told me that is how they survived, and now I can testify to that from firsthand experience.

Sometimes people say they don't want to find meaning in their loss. They just want to call a tragedy a tragedy. To find meaning in it would be to sugarcoat it and they don't want to do that. I think they are afraid that if they let go of the pain, they will lose the connection to their loved one, so I remind them that the pain is theirs and no one can take it away. But if they can find a way to release the pain through meaning, they will still have a deep connection to their child—through love. Just like a broken bone that becomes stronger as it heals, so will their love.

Marriage and Child Loss

The death of a child breaks hearts and, because the pain is so hard to withstand, it can end marriages. We've all heard the dire statistics about some marriages that don't survive the loss of a child. But I don't actually think that marriages end because of the death of a child. I think they end because of how the parents judge each other for not sharing the same feelings they have and not expressing them in the same way.

It's so confusing, because two people in a marriage are sure they know everything about each other. They assume they know how the other person will grieve, and they are shocked at how different it is from what they expected. Maybe the grieving goes on for too long a time, or too short. Maybe they need to talk for hours on end about the child, or maybe they don't want to talk about the death at all. One parent may find comfort going to a group with other bereaved parents. The other parent may be overwhelmed and not want to hear about anybody else's grief.

I remind them that their only job right now is to handle their own grief. They can't really tell their spouse how to deal with their grief. It helps to remember that grief is on the inside and mourning is on the outside. Even though we desperately want to help them, only they can do their inner work. Just as the parents have different relationships with each of their kids and different emotional styles, they will have different experiences of grief. No way of dealing with grief is less legitimate than another.

Joan told me her son, Marty, had cancer for two and a half years. He came home for his treatment, and he was twenty-six when he died. "I feel like I could've made those two and a half years better by getting him out and making him do things," she told me. "But he just wanted to be at home. I feel horrible guilt about that."

Joan's husband, Larry, interrupted, "Stop that, Joan. You made everything as comfortable for him as you possibly could have and were there for him every minute, and that was what he wanted." As we talked more it became apparent that Joan was tormented by everything she felt she had failed to do for Marty during those years, and also by the fact that Larry just couldn't seem to understand why she was so miserable. She was convinced, despite all of her husband's objections, that if only she had been a better mother, she wouldn't have allowed Marty to waste his last years ("waste" is how she viewed it) watching TV and playing video games and rarely leaving the house. Larry didn't see it that way at all. He thought she had been a wonderful, loving mother, and he kept telling her she had to stop beating up on herself. We talked for a while and I suggested to Joan that her son was a typical twenty-three-year-old and he had gotten to do exactly what he wanted to do during his illness—stay home in the sweet safe place she had made for him and distract himself with the kind of entertainments young men of that age enjoy. I told her that I thought she had been an amazing mom. Joan found some comfort from hearing that. But I was also concerned about the disconnect between her and her husband, which I wanted to help them explore.

"Let's get back to Larry," I said. "Joan, how do you feel when all this is going on in your mind and Larry says, 'Stop it'?"

"Like I've been left alone in my grief."

"Larry, do you see now how you allowed her to feel that you had deserted her? Did you mean to do that?"

He answered, "No."

"Of course not. But when you didn't acknowledge what Joan was going through, and you dismissed its importance by telling her to stop torturing herself, she felt abandoned. Larry, your son died. I'm sure it was as devastating for you as it was for Joan. And you may have been feeling abandoned, too, since all of Joan's emotional energy remained focused on Marty at a time when you could have used some love. That's how we leave each other, even when we don't mean to. But neither of you are in the wrong. Your tank is empty and so is hers. You can't expect to heal each other when you're in such pain, and you have to try not to judge each other's grieving."

I explained that each of them would need their own support system, and I asked them questions to help them decide how to create those systems. Which of their friends had had a loss and might understand what they were feeling? Who had shown up for them? Were some friends closer to one of them than to the other? Did they each have work friends who could be counted on? Did they want to seek professional counseling? Was there a church group that would be supportive? Or maybe even a poker group? Or a yoga class? "No judgments," I said. "You can use whatever you want for support. Then when you're together you can be present with each other to share the loss, but you won't feel the need to try to 'fix' each other."

Sex is a frequent source of conflict between grieving parents. At some point after a loss, one person in the marriage may try to initiate sex, while the other may think it's too soon or just not be in the mood. Rebecca said that when her husband, Tim, wanted to have sex a week after their child died, she was shocked. "Our child is in the ground," she said to him, "and you want to pleasure yourself?"

This came up in a support group I was leading, and Tim explained that for him, it wasn't just about pleasure. It was a way of connecting, of being able to feel his wife's love when he needed it so much. But to Rebecca, anything that would be pleasurable felt wrong. For her, just being held would have given her a sense of connection. Another woman told me that when they had sex after her husband's mother died, it was the first time he was able to break down and cry. It released something in him and gave him great relief. You can't make generalizations about what sex means to people. Love, creation, pleasure, connection, release—everyone is different, and at a time of such emotional volatility, what they feel one day may be completely different from the day before.

I worked with another grieving couple who seemed to be communicating across an abyss. The wife told me she felt so lonely in the marriage after their child died that she had recently tried to initiate sex, but her husband rejected her.

"Wait a minute," her husband interrupted. "I tried to have sex with you a month and a half ago and you flew into a rage."

"That was too soon," she snapped.

I asked them to take a time-out so I could talk to each of them separately. I explained to the wife that sex after the loss of a child is confusing and that her husband had no way of knowing when the right time for sex would be. "A month and a half ago it may have been too soon for you, and now it feels too late to him." She needed to express her feelings more openly, but without anger, so they could avoid these misunderstandings. I told the husband something similar, explaining that his wife might be ready for sex one minute and not the next. It wasn't about him. It was about two people not being in the same place in their grief.

When I brought them back together in the same room, I told them that when one person takes the initiative and gets a negative reaction, it's common for both parties to feel hurt and to retreat to their individual corners. But I could see that they were moving toward each other again.

"The fact that sex has become a topic between you," I explained, "means you're getting close to having it again. Even a disagreement about sex is a dance with sex. The ground rule is that if your partner wants to have sex and you don't, you say something like, 'I can't because it hurts too much and I'm too sad, but I love you.' Both of you have to agree to stay present for each other rather than retreating. You can hold each other as a way of being in the moment and offering comfort and love. This is a way to achieve true intimacy when you're grieving. And at some point, guess what happens? Sex happens."

Being a Parent Never Ends

As parents, we talk about our children all the time. We brag about them, complain about them, and make them a focal point of our lives. If you are so unfortunate as to have a child die, you may want to continue to talk about that child all the time—and about your grief for the child. Your friends and family will listen to you for a month, three months, or perhaps even a year, but after a while, they're likely to say that you have to move on.

Moving on is scary because it can feel like you're losing the child all over again. How do we put a time limit on grief? We don't. Most bereaved parents don't understand how many treacherous land mines there are after this kind of loss.

Someone might ask, "How many children do you have?"

How do you answer that? If one child died but you have one or more children who are still alive, how many do you have? If your only child dies, are you still a parent? The answer is yes. Being a parent is an ongoing and never-ending process, even if your child is gone. Our relationships continue after death. But the people around you may think differently, and it may leave you feeling more isolated and alone. That's why it's important to have a place to talk about your losses with people who understand.

There are support groups that focus specifically on bereaved parents, providing a place for them to share stories about their child's life and death. When I attended one of these groups, I saw how openly people were able to talk about their pain without having to rein it in. There was no attempt to question the depth or the duration of the grief because the parents in that room all understood it.

In these groups, there's also an understanding that the connection with the child who died will always be there. People in my online grief groups will often post a child's photo. It might be on the child's birthday or the anniversary of a death. Or it may simply be a random posting because the parent felt like doing it. Outside of these groups, such posts are rare. In your Facebook feed, you may see photos of a mother who died young or a father on Memorial Day in his military uniform who died in a war decades ago, but you rarely find a photo of a child who is deceased. Parents have heard too many times from the outside world that it's time they moved on, so they have learned to keep their grief, and their photos, to themselves. It's sad that they have to fight society for their right to grieve.

Growth by Design

The idea of growth, the sixth stage of meaning, often feels impossible if not unlikely after the death of a child. Yet the reality is that your body, your soul, and your psyche are designed to live again. Richard Tedeschi and Lawrence Calhoun of the University of North Carolina coined the term *posttraumatic growth* in the mid-1990s. "We'd been working with bereaved parents for about a decade," Tedeschi said. "I observed how much they helped each other, how compassionate they were toward other parents whose children had died, and how in the midst of their own grief, they often wanted to do something about changing the circumstances that had contributed to their children's death. Not just for their own satisfaction, but to prevent other families from suffering the kind of loss they were experiencing. These were remarkable and grounded people who were clear about their priorities in life."

They identified five specific ways that people can grow after a tragedy:

1. Their relationships grow stronger.
2. They discover new purposes in life.
3. The trauma allows them to find their inner strength.
4. Their spirituality is deepened.
5. They renew their appreciation for life.

Another helpful concept is how deeply sustaining the ongoing connection can be with the child that only a parent can feel through memories evoked by photos or by talking about the past. Memories are like soft cushions you can fall back on when you need support. My son pops up in my mind a lot and I watch the memories of him almost as I would a movie. I replay them, and I cherish them. Despite my tragic loss, I'm still looking for hope, glimpses of meaning, and for the daylight that might come tomorrow.

CHAPTER TEN

Miscarriage and Infant Loss

I went into the studio and wrote the saddest song I've
ever written in my life.

—Beyoncé

Former First Lady Michelle Obama spoke openly about feeling "lost and alone" after suffering a miscarriage. She said, "I felt like I failed. I didn't know how common miscarriages were because we don't talk about them." That was true twenty years ago when she miscarried, and it's true to this day. We have done far too little to destigmatize miscarriage. Even our dictionaries often include the word "failure" in the definition.

One of the keys to ending this feeling of self-blame is to know that miscarriages, just like any other death, happen and they aren't anyone's fault. Mrs. Obama said, "We sit in our own pain, thinking that somehow we're broken. I think the worst thing that we do to each other as women is to not share the truth about our bodies and how they work."

Miscarriage and infant loss are often minimized. Since there are a lot of different beliefs about when life actually begins, the loss is complicated by how our society views pregnancy loss, stillbirth, and infant death. On an emotional level, the mother begins a connection with her unborn child the moment she knows she's pregnant—or, as we say, that she's "expecting." The same emotional connection is true for the father. When something goes wrong, they are faced with the reality of loss. How can they say goodbye when they've never had a chance to say hello? They are grieving for what could have been. But those around them are often insensitive to the depth of their feelings.

Maureen had never thought about the possibly of having a miscarriage. Her first son's birth was "easy breezy," so when she became pregnant again, she expected the same. She told me:

My first son, Jimmy, was three and we were all thrilled that a new child was on its way. I had been watching my cycle pretty closely, so I knew immediately when I was pregnant. I was feeling the normal first trimester stuff, but after eight or nine weeks, I woke up with this migraine headache and saw I had spotting.

My doctor told me to come to the hospital clinic for an ultrasound, just to check things out. I went in by myself. Looking back now, that wasn't a good idea. When they told me there was no heartbeat, I was crushed. I had bonded with this baby, I was sobbing, and the ultrasound technician had no idea what to say. She had initially made fun small talk about the baby, but now after looking at the screen, she was silent.

They moved me to the OB-GYN department in the hospital and put me in a little room. The nurse came in and verified my name and birth date and left. She obviously didn't know what to say even though she worked in OB-GYN and must surely have seen other women who had gone through this.

Another nurse came in and I was sobbing. "I don't know what to do now," I said. "Do I bury it? What happens next?"

"It's just a small sack of cells," the nurse said quite matter-of-factly.

I was horrified. This was a baby I was decorating a room for and changing my life for. It was a loved one inside of me. When the nurse told me they would be scheduling me for a D and C, I asked again, "What happens to the remains?"

"It's just medical waste," she said.

Afterward my heart was broken but I didn't tell any of my friends, even though they had all known I was pregnant. Then one day I had to take my son to a birthday party for one of his playmates and I knew my friends would be there and I'd have to tell them. I didn't know how they would take the news. At a certain point, when we were in a room away from the kids, I started crying. My friends all stopped and asked me what was going on.

I told them I'd had a miscarriage. When I said that I didn't know what I'd done wrong, they reassured me that it wasn't because of anything I had done. It just happens. Turned out that quite a few of them had had miscarriages before they had their kids and in between their kids. It was healing to know that I wasn't the only one, but I wondered why we hadn't talked about it before. Why didn't I know?

One friend said, "It's a thing no one talks about until you have to talk about it." I think it would be better if we opened up about this much more than we do.

For Maureen, talking about miscarriage with her friends was important. It brought a feeling of connection, and with that a sense of meaning. "It's strange that such a horrible loss can connect us to one another," she said, but she now feels closer to her friends and to her husband as well.

Unseen Losses

The pain caused by the secrecy and silence that surround miscarriage, as well as the loss of a child in early infancy, is incalculable, making what would already have been excruciating to bear even more so. I had an eye-opening conversation about this with Dr. Donna Schuurman, the senior director of advocacy and training and former executive director at the Dougy Center for Grieving Children & Families in Portland, Oregon.

Donna began, "I started at the Dougy Center in 1991. People were always asking me, 'Did you have a loss that drew you to this work?'

"I told them that a lot of leaders of grief organizations do have dramatic stories about what made them start, but not me. I volunteered there because it sounded like a good cause, and when their executive director left, I was on the board and I ultimately applied and got the job.

"During my ten years of work here, I never thought about my own family history of grief and loss. I had grown up knowing that my mother had a child before me, and that the baby had died, but we were taught that we weren't supposed to ask about it."

For reasons she can't explain, however, one day Donna called her mother to ask about the baby she had lost:

I'm not sure what my impetus was at the time, but I wanted to know the story. My mother grew up Irish, in a staunch "Buck up, don't share your dirty laundry, life is rough" kind of family. I called her fearfully. I didn't think she would hang up, but I thought she might say, "I don't want to talk about it. It was a long time ago."

"Mom," I told her. "I've been thinking about your life. I don't know if you want to talk about it, but if you do, I'd like to hear the story about your first child, who would've been my sister."

Three hours later, I hung up the phone. She had launched into the story and it turned out that nobody had ever asked her to talk about it. There was a lot of shame involved. My mother was eighteen and my father was nineteen when the baby was born. She was born alive with her heart outside of her body and she died five days after birth. After the death my mother's father said to my parents, "We took care of everything."

To this day, my mother doesn't know what they did. Did they bury the five-day-old infant? Did they cremate her? My mother has no idea. According to her, she and my father never spoke of their first child for the rest of their lives. After that, my two brothers and I were born.

That conversation with my mother opened not just a dialogue, but a communication between the two of us that I can't define in words. It unleashed something that made us closer. It was meaningful to see her as a vulnerable human being and not just my mother. I was able to picture that eighteen-year-old girl grieving the death of her baby without anyone to talk to or offer her support or love. Our conversation opened something in her, too. Today she's almost ninety. She lives in an apartment back east near my oldest brother and now she often talks about her baby. My mother said that she had tried to decrease her own pain and find some meaning around it by realizing that if Lynne, her daughter, had lived, maybe she wouldn't have had me.

My parents divorced after forty years of marriage. When I asked my mom when she knew the marriage was over, she said, "Do you want to know the truth?"

"Yes."

"It was over for me when I came home from the hospital without the baby and we could never talk about it."

She never got a birth certificate for the baby. She just got a death certificate. It was like the baby didn't count, and she felt ashamed. "I was an eighteen-year-old healthy girl. How could I have had a deformed baby? You know, it was shaming, like it must have happened because of me."

Donna's story shows how much pain lies beneath the surface of families who live in secrecy after such losses, and how much damage it can do. It also reveals something about the pain caused by our lack of communal rituals to commemorate these losses.

Another woman, Elyse, told me about suffering a miscarriage twenty years ago, and how hard it is for her to this day that she has almost nothing to show she was ever pregnant. The lack of any physical evidence has been particularly hard for her because after she lost the baby, she discovered she had severe endometriosis and had to have a hysterectomy, which meant she could never bear a child. Like Donna's mother, she wasn't given a birth certificate. She wasn't even given a death certificate. "If a baby didn't take a breath back then," she told me, "they weren't considered alive. We wanted to have something in print about the miscarriage, but the newspaper would not allow me to do an obituary."

Other than an ultrasound picture that had been taken she had no proof that her baby ever existed. But there was one thing she did have, which was a source of great meaning to her—a gravesite she could visit. "Fortunately, where I was in Indiana, the hospital did burials for miscarriages up to twenty weeks. They used a common casket and they would put the remains of each inside that casket. I could go to the cemetery and I could actually see where they had buried Jeff.

"At the common grave, I met other women who were struggling with the same loss I was. It gave me incredible compassion for them. Helping them and being able to talk about what we had been through brought meaning and connection to all of our losses."

Elyse's words touch on a recurring theme I've heard in discussions with many women who have lost a child, either in early infancy or by miscarriage, which is how connected they feel to the child and what an enduring connection it is. For Elyse, who was never able to have another child because of her hysterectomy, Mother's Day is still a challenge all these years later. "Am I a mother, or am I not a mother? When asked, I always respond with, 'Yes, I'm a mother of a child who would've been nineteen, if he were still alive.'" Over the years she has thought about each of the milestones he would be passing—walking, saying his first words, entering kindergarten, grade school, then middle school, learning to drive, etc. "Boy, he'd be almost a high school graduate now! I think about that as I continue to raise him in my heart."

Another woman, a colleague of mine, Melo Garcia, gave birth to a child preterm, at only twenty-four weeks, and weighing only 1.9 pounds. She, too, retains a deep connection to her child, and during Chloe's very brief life, which was spent in a neonatal intensive care unit, she and her husband felt they really got to know their daughter, and she them.

"Chloe was the greatest love I think I'll ever have. It was devastating to watch her trying so desperately to live, but it was also a huge realization about the gift of life. Whenever her father or I would walk into the room, her heart rate would go up, especially when she would hear or see her dad. Even on the day that she died, her little heart beat faster when her dad touched her. I knew she wanted more than anything to stay alive to be with us. She loved us, and we loved her."

This was a profound and meaningful relationship, no matter how brief, and it changed Melo. "I realized that I couldn't mess around with this life that I was given. I don't take it for granted anymore. When little Chloe was dying in her father's arms, I promised her I was going to do my best and I would honor her in everything that I did. Today I try to remind people that this life is a gift. We should enjoy it because when it's gone, it's gone. We don't have a promised time. We're not given do-overs, so we better appreciate it now.

"Later I started an organization called After Chloe. Its mission is Let's Find Your After. I wanted people to understand that we can live after loss. That's not to say that you shouldn't grieve your loss. It's not about taking anything away from it. It's about honoring the love that remains and living the best life we can. That's become the bottom line for everything I do."

Meaning through Vocation

When I was doing a training for professionals, I noticed a young man, Nicolas, who was taking lots of notes. At lunch, I asked, "What kind of work do you do?"

"I'm a funeral director. I just graduated from mortuary school."

"Congratulations. What are you hoping to learn here today?"

"I really want to know as much as I can about grief and loss."

"What brought you into this field?" I asked.

"When I was in college, I worked in a funeral home. It was a side job. I was planning on a career in tech, but I made a change."

"Tech to mortuary school is a big change. What happened?"

"My wife was pregnant," he said with tears in his eyes, "and she had a miscarriage."

"That must have been so hard for you."

"That's something you don't hear every day," he said. "That's why I wanted to be here today. Few people said what you just said."

"That it's hard for you?"

"Yes. Most people assume it's fine for the dad and focus on the mom. My wife knew how much I was looking forward to this child. So when people would tell her that they were so sorry for her loss and ignore me, she'd grab my hand in front of them and say how hard it had been for *both* of us."

"Sounds like you have a wonderful wife," I said.

"I do. We shared our grief and both of us understood how painful it was to lose our baby. That's why I'm doing the work I do now."

"Which is what?" I asked.

"I work with parents who have lost premature babies or very young infants. I focus on the preparation side. I spend time making the baby look good, so they have a good last image. I can do a lot to make them presentable. The parents have so little time to be with the baby, I want them to have a beautiful last memory. When I ask them if they can bring in any baby clothes, their mothers are surprised. 'You can dress my baby?' they say. 'Isn't a premature baby too small for clothes?' I tell them to bring them in and I will make them work."

"That's so important," I said. "Are there other things you do to help?"

"I do hand- and footprints. That's something they can take with them. They have so little evidence of the life of their baby."

Nicolas understands that after an infant loss or miscarriage, parents will find meaning in memories that have a physical representation.

The Medical World Is Changing

Few people, even those in the caring professions, have grasped how important it is for parents to have the bond with their babies honored. But in recent years this has begun to change. Naomi, a nurse who was attending one of my lectures, shared how her hospital now deals with late miscarriages, stillbirths, and infant deaths. It used to be that the body of a baby who was stillborn or died shortly after birth was removed immediately, as if the sooner forgotten, the better. Today, hospitals like Naomi's are adopting protocols that allow mothers and fathers to spend time with their dead child, for hours or sometimes even days, in order to make memories. This may sound odd. But when parents are left with no evidence that they ever had a child, the grief that follows such a death can be very complicated. "All the labor, delivery, and neonatal intensive care units and the units at her hospital have cameras for the parents to take pictures.

The other problem is that babies' bodies deteriorate much more quickly than adults'. The hospital would have to take the baby to the morgue, then bring it back for parents to see. Now things have dramatically changed with new cribs that keep the baby's body stable. It is a small portable refrigeration system that allows the baby to stay next to mom and family in a beautiful crib. They look more like sleeping angels than babies brought up from the morgue.

Naomi recently worked with Hannah, the mother of twins. At twenty-eight weeks, Hannah gave birth to William, who lived, and Dylan who didn't. It can be confusing when joy and sorrow occur together. Baby William was taken immediately after birth to the neonatal intensive care unit, where he would remain for several weeks until he was strong enough to go home, while the stillborn baby, Dylan, was brought into the delivery room to be with Hannah. She wanted to bathe him and dress him, which her husband, Noah, thought was very strange.

When Noah watched her do this, he became upset and told her, "Focus on our living baby, William. Stop thinking about this baby."

"Stop thinking?" she said. "Is that what you think this is? Tears come from the heart, not the brain. This isn't about what I'm thinking. This is what I need to do." She began to cry when he admonished her, and the hospital staff educated Noah about the importance of her being able to express her feelings for the child they had lost. Naomi explained, "For many mothers, the act of holding their babies, skin to skin, has a great deal of meaning. Dressing and bathing is their one chance to parent." These are the only moments where they can make memories. Mothers are initially so consumed with the miracle of childbirth they need time to take it in. We need to give the parent time before we expect them to let go."

This helped Noah understand his wife's reaction, but he wanted to spare Hannah any further pain by removing one of the two cribs they had set up at home. He intended to do this before Hannah left the hospital, but the staff suggested he check in with her first. When he did, she told him not to remove the crib, she wanted to be there when it left. She wanted to be a part of it.

Once Hannah came home, Noah said, "Can we take it down now?"

"Not yet," she said. "I need a few days."

During a visit to William in the neonatal ICU, Noah told the hospital staff that he was upset that the crib was still there. But they explained that to Hannah, the crib was about the baby who was supposed to sleep in it, and she wasn't yet ready to say goodbye to it. Noah wondered how long they were going to have to look at this empty crib, which to him was just a reminder of heartbreak.

For Hannah, letting go of the crib occurred organically—and meaningfully. One day when she was at the neonatal ICU, she overheard a woman whose baby had also arrived early tell a nurse that she didn't have the money to buy a crib for when the baby would come home.

"I have a crib for you," Hannah said. "My husband will be glad to bring it over." And he was.

CHAPTER ELEVEN

Illnesses of Our Mind: Mental Illness and Addiction

My mind is a bad neighborhood. I try not to go into it alone.

—Anne Lamott

Why do I put mental illness and addiction in the same chapter? Because they're both illnesses that occur in our minds, and because they often occur in the same person. To be clear, not every person with an addiction has a mental illness and not every person with a mental illness has an addiction, but, according to the National Institute on Drug Abuse, there are inherent links between them. Those with mental illnesses are twice as likely to develop a substance abuse problem. The medical term often used is "dual diagnosis." While they may manifest differently, they are both progressive illnesses that will get worse if untreated and may result in death.

When someone has died from addiction or mental illness (including the mental illnesses that result in suicide), there's a great temptation to judge the person. People will often say inappropriate things about such deaths that they would never say about anyone who died of a physical disease. For example:

In Mental Illness and Addiction, the Sufferer:	In Physical Illness, the Sufferer:
Gets blamed.	Gets cared for.
Is told, "Get over it."	Is told, "You'll be supported through it."
Is told, "Take responsibility for your problems."	Is told, "Don't blame yourself."
Is told, "Stop seeking attention."	Is told, "Ask for help anytime."
Is criticized for being weak and lazy.	Is praised for being strong and courageous.
Is told, "Stop being so self-indulgent."	Is told, "It's a hard road. Be kind to yourself."
Is told, "It's a choice."	Is told, "There's nothing you could have done to avoid this."

The messages to those suffering from mental illness and addiction are wrong. If a mentally ill person could stop the voices in her head that are urging her to harm herself or others, she would. If an addict could shake his habit and stop using drugs or alcohol, he would, especially if he understood it could lead to his death.

At a talk I gave recently, someone said, as people so often do, "Addiction is a choice."

I don't believe addiction to drugs or alcohol is any more of a choice than addiction to tobacco and nicotine. If someone gets lung cancer, we *could* say it's their fault for smoking. But society is beginning to reconsider its thinking about that. I started smoking when I was thirteen. The movies I watched, the commercials on TV, and the billboards on the highways told me I would be cool if I smoked. So I did, for twenty-seven years. I tried to quit over and over again, and I was unsuccessful. I couldn't understand how someone as aware and determined as I was couldn't break the habit. I finally quit for good some years ago, but the struggle taught me something about the nature of addiction, its physical hold and the societal and economic factors that reinforce it.

Thanks to a major lawsuit brought by the American Cancer Society and others against Big Tobacco, here are just a few of the truths we understand about how the tobacco companies encouraged smoking—despite knowing how harmful it is:

- Altria, R. J. Reynolds Tobacco, Lorillard, and Philip Morris USA intentionally designed cigarettes to make them more addictive.
- Cigarette companies control the impact and delivery of nicotine, the addictive agent in cigarettes, in many ways, including designing filters and selecting cigarette paper to maximize the ingestion of nicotine.
- When you smoke, the nicotine actually changes the brain. That's why quitting is so hard.

We are responsible for our health. But I also believe that we're not to blame for our illnesses. I'm speaking specifically about addictions. When our loved ones die from addiction, it's fair to say they had a part to play in their deaths, but they weren't alone. Big business—in other words, greed—plays a huge part, not just in our nicotine addiction but in the current opioid epidemic, which involves prescription pain relievers, heroin, and synthetic opioids such as fentanyl.

I always had great respect for my namesake, David Kessler, who was head of the Food and Drug Administration (FDA). He was known for his fight against the tobacco industry and obesity, and he seemed to put the public's health first. Once he left the FDA, the appropriate labeling on strong pain-relieving medication was expanded. It was no longer used just for short-term pain as it had been intended. Now, anyone with any pain could get them. I had only known these medications in hospice and palliative care that were used appropriately for the dying. Now they could be widely prescribed as well as overprescribed. In the strangest twist of fate, one David Kessler leaving the FDA would indirectly play a role in the death of my son, another David Kessler.

In the late 1990s, pharmaceutical companies reassured the medical community that patients would not become addicted to opioid pain relievers and health care providers began to prescribe them more frequently. One purveyor was Purdue Pharma, which sold tens of billions of dollars of OxyContin, a pain-reliever opioid they knew to be addictive. More than seven million Americans are estimated to have abused Oxy-Contin, and the states with the highest rates of OxyContin abuse also had the largest increase in heroin deaths. That is partly because many of those addicted to OxyContin switched to heroin, a cheaper opioid, when they could no longer afford the steadily rising price of OxyContin.

In "The Opioid Diaries," a special issue of *Time* magazine that was published in 2018, John, a drug user in Massachusetts, described how he ended up on heroin:

> I'm an addict. I had a career in sales in the automobile business. I was making a lot of money, upward of $100,000 a year. Then I started up with the OxyContin. It's an amazing feeling, that warm hug from Jesus. It started as a once-in-a-while thing. But I began telling myself, "Well, if I can feel this good on Friday and Saturday, why shouldn't I feel this good on Tuesday and Wednesday?" And then the price started going up, and all of a sudden, they're $80 a pill. At this point, I've got a six- or seven-pills-a-day habit. I wouldn't get out of bed without one. I always knew about heroin, but it was a line I didn't want to cross. But, you know, the ship had already sailed. An opiate's an opiate. I'm not trying to die, contrary to people's belief. I'm not trying to kill myself. I'm just an addict.

The other David Kessler has now publicly come out against his own former agency, the FDA. Purdue and other pharmaceutical companies put profits before our loved ones' lives. I think in decades to come, we are going to look back and see addiction very differently. It will seem absurdly flawed that we put all the blame on the addict, given how many other forces contributed to the problem.

Fighting the Stigma

Addiction should no longer be seen as a moral failing or a lack of willpower. It is a medical problem, an illness that leads to a progressively worsening chronic condition, and one that is particularly hard to fight, because the drugs involved attack the brain of users, the very organ that helps us fight other dangers to our survival. The same can be said for mental illness. We can't tell a person who is mentally ill or addicted to use his brain to help himself recover, because his brain *is* the diseased organ. Because such people cannot do what is necessary to help themselves, professional help is necessary but often hard to find, or expensive, or not very good, or some combination of all of the above. Even the best of help often fails, which is why people relapse so often after rehab and sometimes die of an overdose or suicide. Addiction and mental illness are afflictions that last a lifetime. Dealing with them will be an ongoing battle.

Yet the stigma associated with people suffering from these afflictions remains. "Isn't it their fault? Didn't they choose it? Couldn't they have prevented it by taking their pills or going to a twelve-step meeting?" These are the kinds of questions that arise. Those who don't ask them have often suffered the loss of a loved one, and they are more likely to say things like, "I used to agree with people who said they have a choice . . . until I watched my brother fight this terrible illness."

Mental illness and addiction are present in all walks of life. People who have suffered trauma from any number of causes including sexual abuse, child abuse, and domestic violence are among those particularly at risk. So, too, are the men and women who have fought in this country's wars. It's one thing to absolve them of blame for their subsequent problems. It can be even harder to find meaning in these troubled lives.

Miranda told the story of her husband, Andy, who was a Vietnam vet. "He experienced a wartime tragedy and often spoke about the deaths he had witnessed there. After the war he ended up with an addiction to medication he'd been prescribed for back pain."

Her eyes teared up as she continued.

In our early years together, my husband seemed okay. He worked at the family locksmith business, he was functional, and the business was successful. As his back pain worsened, he started to show signs of paranoia and began using drugs more heavily. The trouble reared its ugly head at nighttime. He would become agitated and I would find him going through drawers or pulling the couch apart. He was digging through everything for no apparent reason. As his addiction got worse over the next few years, I would find him sitting underneath his desk, afraid that somebody was coming after him. It broke my heart to see this once strong man being broken by his mind. He went to a couple of rehabilitation centers and he stopped using for a while. But then he started again.

I came home one day, and I knew Andy was high and had locked himself inside the house. I called his counselor from the rehabilitation center. "What should I do?" I asked her.

She said, "Pack his bags and come back here."

I got him to open the door and I said, "I think you need to go back there."

When I told his counselor that he refused, she said, "If he doesn't stop using, he'll die. Bring him to the hospital."

I found him standing naked in the bedroom and he told me he was burning up. He was obviously intoxicated, and I said, "I need to get you to the hospital."

He agreed to go, but when I was helping him put on his

shorts, he had a seizure and lost consciousness. I called 911. When the paramedics were taking him out on the gurney, my husband's heart stopped. At age thirty-seven, he died of an accidental drug overdose right there.

I was thirty-two at the time and my life turned completely upside down. I had two children, seven and four years old, and until then I had been mainly a stay-at-home mom. At first I went to a counseling center in town that had support groups for me and my children. Later I went to Al-Anon meetings [which offer support for the families and friends of alcoholics and all other addicts]. I wanted to make something of my life, not just for myself but for my children who had lost their father.

The work I had to do to make that possible was profound. It was in Al-Anon that I began to understand the role I had played in Andy's problems, but more important, the role I didn't play.

In Al-Anon they talk about the "three C's." For those who love someone with an addiction problem, the three C's can help them to understand the limits of their responsibility:

1. We didn't *cause* it.
2. We cannot *control* it.
3. We cannot *cure* it.

Knowing this is important during life with an addict, and even more so after an addict's death. It doesn't change what happened, but it helps stop the self-blaming.

Miranda continues:

Although Andy had talked some about what he'd gone through in Vietnam, I hadn't realized how traumatized he had been. After he died, I discovered that for years he had kept a storage locker with journals in which he wrote about things from his past. Reading them I understood a lot more about what happened to him there. One story stands out in my mind. When he was fighting in Vietnam, he witnessed people riding their bikes over dead bodies that were laid out like shrimp in the streets. He couldn't get it out of his mind.

I finally realized that Andy had died of mental illness caused by the traumatic experiences he'd had in the war. His mind tried to handle the pain by numbing it with alcohol and opiates, but the effects never lasted long enough. Understanding why he had become addicted was important to me and to our children. It meant that their father was not a bad man or a failure. He was a courageous, brave man who had served his country. I had to see him that way, and it was the truth that changed everything. If he'd been shot, the army would have given him a purple heart. But because his fatal wound took the form of mental illness and addiction, it was on the inside where it couldn't be seen.

On the first anniversary of Andy's death, we gathered at his grave and had a ceremony. We each said what good parts of him we will keep alive in the future. Then we laid a wreath of purple flowers we had bought on his grave. It was us, the people who knew him, who gave him a purple heart. That's what I'm keeping alive in my thoughts about Andy—his purple heart. We found meaning by understanding that he was not a victim but an unsung hero in the Vietnam War.

Rejecting the stigma associated with addiction and trauma and shifting her perception allowed Miranda to see her husband for the person he was. His life had real meaning, and she was able to honor him for who he was and what he had done for his country.

Meaning Is Everywhere—If You Look

When a loved one suffers from mental illness or addiction, your grief often begins long before death. You grieve for the loss of the future you had imagined living with that person, for the terrible changes that have overtaken the person, and for the nightmare you watch unfolding, which keeps getting worse and worse. Yet sometimes even in the midst of that suffering there is meaning to be found for both you and your loved one. To be able to share meaning with someone who is still living and breathing is a rare gift.

A psychologist, Margaret, told me this story:

My sister, Cynthia, suffered from schizophrenia her whole adult life. When she was eighteen, in art school she had a psychotic break in the backseat of a car when friends were driving her home. When they were about to drop her off, she began screaming and hollering so loudly that people in nearby houses could all hear her. Suddenly she didn't recognize anyone and kept crying for her mother, who had run out to the car to get her and was right by her side. "You're not my mom," she said over and over. She didn't know where she was or what was going on. I was thirteen and I saw the whole thing, which was really shocking. It had such an impact on me that years later, it influenced my decision to become a psychotherapist.

After her breakdown, Cynthia was admitted to a psychiatric hospital where she stayed for a long time until they were able to find the right mix of drugs to treat her. When she came out, she was much better and was able to get a place of her own and find a job working for an art supply store in town. She went to college part time, where she loved studying art and languages, and where she met her husband, who was a professor of archaeology. She was still plagued by her schizophrenia, but the medications seemed to keep it under control. For a while, things seemed good. She went on archaeological digs with her husband and drew the illustrations for his articles, books, and research papers. However, her husband never gave her credit for her work and after a few years, they got a divorce.

From there things went downhill. No longer able to work, my sister went on disability and she lived in poverty. One day she found a lump in her breast, but she told no one and delayed going to the doctor because she was terrified about what he would find. By the time she went, it was too late. She had stage IV cancer. Because she couldn't take care of herself, she came to live with my husband and me. I'd always wanted my sister back, but not this way. It was so sad. She knew she was dying, and one day she told me that she felt her life had been completely meaningless.

I told her I didn't agree with that. She was my inspiration, the reason I became a psychotherapist. She had helped thousands of people because she had inspired me. This talk changed how she looked at her life. She didn't know she had been my inspiration. It had never occurred to her that she had contributed anything to the world. "Maybe my life was worth something after all," she said, and that seemed to make her happy.

This change in her point of view allowed her to stop ruminating about having wasted her life. She was able to settle in and deal with dying. By the time she died about a month later, I felt like I had my sister back—my real sister, not the illness.

Margaret's love for her sister allowed both of them to find some meaning during her final days. But it's understandable that the challenges of supporting a mentally ill or drug-addicted family member can sometimes seem overwhelming. There's a compassion fatigue that sets in after multiple episodes of having to come to someone's rescue.

A few years ago, my friend Beth confided her exasperation with having to deal with her eighty-year-old father who had just overdosed again and had been put on a ventilator in the hospital. Her father was bipolar and had a longstanding problem with drug addiction. Over the years, Beth had to fly home repeatedly to help her father when he was hospitalized due to an overdose or locked up in the psych unit after a breakdown.

This time Beth was dealing with her own problems because she and her husband had divorced a year ago and she was trying to raise three young children on her own.

"David," she said, "when I first got the call that Dad was hospitalized, I was in tears, thinking this was it and he was dying and I was ready to get on the first plane to go see him. However, when the next call came, and they told me he was off the ventilator, breathing on his own and was likely to recover, I thought, 'For what? He'll just end up going through this again in another couple of months when he overdoses or makes another suicide attempt.' I felt guilty thinking that, but it's been so challenging over the years. And now, with my father who doesn't even seem to want to stay alive, it's a lot to handle. If he doesn't care about living, why should I care whether he lives or dies? His life just seems meaningless."

Beth asked me what advice I could offer her. I wanted to witness her pain and acknowledge how hard her situation was, but I also wanted to spare her the self-blaming she might feel in the future if she allowed her anger to prevent her from saying a meaningful farewell.

"As much as you have every right to think, 'not again,' just know that this might be a time to say goodbye to your dad," I said. "Whether he eventually dies by suicide or by an accidental overdose, your dad is ultimately dying of mental illness. I think if you acknowledge that fact, it will be easier for you to feel sympathy for him and deal with the reality that your dad's life is winding down."

Focusing on the idea that this might be her last chance to be with her dad allowed Beth to overcome her anger and spend some meaningful time with him during his final days. "Now that he has been gone a few years," Beth said, "I'm so grateful that we had that time together and that I was able to find some love and sympathy for him."

When we believe the person has a hand in taking the action that ends his or her life, it's hard to see the big picture. But no matter how it comes about, it's still the end for that person. If it's someone we care about, we help both the person who is dying and ourselves by being there. If we aren't, there may be a lot of guilt and self-recrimination afterward.

Making Meaning from Addiction

In this area, I'm not just the grief expert reporting on these types of events. I've lived through them. My son David was born drug exposed and had been in multiple foster homes before I adopted him. Once he and his brother came to live with me, he adjusted well and was a really sweet kid. In kindergarten he was voted the most likely to go into a caring profession. He cared about his school work and his friends. He was bright, articulate, and made straight A's. However, he was a sensitive child who suffered from feeling different from everyone else because of being adopted. The fact that he was being raised by a single parent—who was a man—also made him feel different. Like most kids, he just wanted to fit in and be like everybody else.

At the private school he was attending, he was bullied by many of the kids in his grade when he was fifteen. Like a lot of kids who are bullied, he didn't tell his father and I wasn't aware of it, even though I was on the school board. Later it came out that some of the teachers had known about the bullying and had gone to the administration, but those who were in charge failed to act. The bullying became so unbearable to David that one day he went into the bathroom at school and took a handful of his brother's heart medication. His Spanish teacher found him unresponsive in the bathroom with a note that said he couldn't take it anymore. Luckily, the ambulance arrived quickly, and he was transported to the local hospital where he recovered. But the bullying triggered something in him, and he found it hard to rebound. He became deeply depressed and needed a lot of psychological support. One night he came running to me in tears, with his brother, Richard, by his side. "Dad," David said, "the voices in my head are telling me to hurt myself and to hurt you."

That was an excruciating moment, seeing my innocent fifteen-year-old son crying and desperately frightened by the voices in his head. Richard and I stayed up with David all night, reassuring him that we were not going to let the voices get through to him. During those long hours with David, I came face-to-face with the true depth of pain in mental illness and trauma, which is every bit as intense as any physical pain. Together, we all fought the voices in his head that night, and in the morning I took him to his psychiatrist, who adjusted his medications. That, along with intensive psychotherapy and group work, seemed to help David get his feet back on the ground. He started high school at a private Catholic school and did well for a while.

David began volunteering in the emergency room in the hospital where I was working. He loved helping people and began to consider a career in medicine. He did ride-alongs with the paramedics and could talk for hours about what happened there and in the emergency room. The more complicated the case, the more interesting for him. He spent nine days attending the National Youth Leadership Forum on Medicine at UCLA medical school, which was a program for future doctors and health care practitioners to discover their passions through hands-on experience.

As much as he was excited about what the future had in store for him, he was still fighting demons from his past. Trauma and mental health challenges are complicated. When they are exacerbated by drug addiction, they can be life-threatening. The same way I had the opportunity to drink a beer and smoke some pot as a teenager, so did David, but for him the risks were greater—and some of the drugs available to him were far more dangerous. When he was sixteen, he tried crystal meth for the first time. He got high with some friends and called me from a neighborhood park. He knew immediately that he was in over his head.

We then entered an unknown world that seemed to be sucking us under. I could feel David sinking. He went overnight from choosing a college to choosing a rehab. His college funds were redirected to rehabs. The world seemed to be changing fast, and David was changing with it.

For the two years before David turned eighteen, we were struggling to keep him sober. I knew when he hit the age of eighteen, my influence would drastically diminish. Each period of his sobriety was followed by a relapse. This was a problem that love, time, or money couldn't solve. There were multiple rehabs, outpatient programs, and therapy. It seemed to be a mountain that none of us could climb. The lure of the drugs was too strong and David's best efforts to stay off them seemed to fall short. At one point I heard that David had tried heroin. It was cheap, easy to get, and apparently was a high that made all the pain go away.

Once when he was trying out a new twelve-step recovery program, someone said to him, "I hope you have a black suit. You're going to be going to a lot of funerals." I was horrified at that thought, but I acknowledged the truth of it. I had noticed an increase in bereaved parents attending my lectures. One night, David and I were talking and I told him, "At every lecture, I see all these heartbroken parents. I'm glad you're not using anymore. Promise me I'll never be one of those parents."

"You won't," he assured me. "Even when I was using, I knew what I was doing."

On one hand, I believed him, he would not be one of the tragic deaths I was hearing about. And at the same time, it was not reassuring. I don't think any addict knows what he's up against when he's using. I remember an exchange I had had with a facilitator at the first rehab David went to. I had gone to one of the meetings where they invited parents to join them, and I was shocked to hear how casually some of the people who were there for treatment talked about other addicts who had overdosed. Later I said to the facilitator, "I don't understand how they can talk so flippantly about overdoses. How can any of them think they're not in the same danger as the people who died?"

The facilitator responded, "Addiction is about numbness. When you're addicted, that numbness allows you to ignore the danger, to think that you're in control when you're using. And even when you get sober, you may still be numb to the danger and relapse. We understand that relapse is part of recovery."

"Not if it ends in death," I had said at the time. And that worried me.

His first years of adulthood were about David being sober and just functioning in the world. The articulate boy who was considering a career in medicine was trying to see if he could hold down a job. When that didn't work out, he attended an adult extension program at UCLA to be a paramedic. But his efforts collapsed under the weight of addiction. He would later enter Los Angeles Community College, but obviously, my son's recovery didn't go as planned.

In my grief, I was haunted by that exchange I'd had with the facilitator at the rehab facility about addiction and numbness. I kept replaying it in my mind, until I began to wonder if there was something I could do to penetrate that numbness in other young addicts, to give them a wake-up call about the danger they were courting. This would be one thing I could do to ensure that David had not died in vain.

A year after David's death, I went to see a colleague who ran a sober living home in Los Angeles. I told him about my concerns and said that I would like to brainstorm a plan with him for how to help the recovering addicts who were in his care.

About three months later, I met with fifteen young men at the funeral home that had arranged for my son's burial. Their ages ranged from twenty to thirty and they looked guarded. They had no idea why they were at a funeral home or what to expect. Then I showed them a five-minute video clip about David's life, which at first seemed to be just a home movie about a little boy growing up, not anything that would be of interest to anyone who wasn't part of the family. But when it

began to show David in his late teenage years and early twen-
ties, they saw him standing outside a twelve-step meeting, chat-
ting with his friends. I could see it beginning to click. "Oh, he's
just like us," they were probably thinking. In the next moment,
someone saw a friend of his in the video. The energy in the
room shifted visibly and I could see that it was becoming real
for them. The video ended with David blowing out the candles
on a cake on his twenty-first birthday.

Someone in the video shouted, "Speech!"

"I'm taking it one day at a time," David said. That's something you hear a lot in AA and other recovery programs. The
video faded to black, and on the screen, there was a one-
sentence epilogue stating that David died of an accidental overdose sixteen days later. I could see from the guys' faces that
David had become a person they could relate to.

I asked them, "How many of you expected to be at a funeral
home today?"

No one raised his hand.

"Well, a year ago neither did I," I said. "But a few days after
seeing my son for the last time, I found myself in this very
funeral home."

Then we headed up to the cemetery, a short walk from the
funeral home. When we arrived at David's gravesite, I asked
them each to reach into a box and take one of the stones I had
put there, which were inscribed with different words: Peace.
Happiness. Family. Love. Compassion. Acceptance. I explained
that in the Jewish religion, it's customary to bring stones to
the cemetery instead of flowers. Then I asked the young men
to place the stones, one by one, on David's grave and read the
words aloud as they did so. After they placed each stone, I
explained how the word related to David's life. When one of
the young men read the stone that said Hope, I said, "David
had a lot of hope for his future." The next man's stone said
Family, and I told them, "David loved the idea of family, but he
still wasn't sure where he belonged." For the next stone, Love,
I said, "Despite so much love in David's life, he never felt loved.

Everyone agreed that he would have been shocked at the number of people who attended his funeral."

As we stood at David's grave, one of the men asked, "How do you get through an event like this?"

"It's not an event," I said. "It's the rest of my life."

And that's the truth. I'll be grieving for David Jr. for the rest of my life. But I will also be trying to make some meaning out of my loss—by being of service. I turned to the guys and said, "I hope that the next time one of your parents or friends says to you, 'I'm so afraid that with your addiction you might die,' you won't roll your eyes. Your addiction is a cunning and baffling disease that could result in your death. If David had reached out for help when he was tempted to do drugs again, he might still be here. But this is not about blame. At the end of the day, David's addiction, and his addiction alone, killed him. When you consider using again, I hope this visit will remind you what's at stake."

After I gave them a few more details about David's life, his recovery, and his relapse, I said, "David is not allowed possessions here at the cemetery. The staff comes through every so often and picks up all the flowers and stones. Anything left behind, they remove. The stones we placed on David's grave are not for him. They're for you." I asked them, one by one, to pick up their stone and share how the word on the stone related to their own lives.

The first young man picked up the stone that read Family. He said, "I'm always in conflict with my family. I never thought about how much fear they might have over what could happen to me."

The next man's stone said Hope. He shared that he often feels hopeless about life. I said to him, "If there's one thing I want you to take away from today, it's that when you think of using again, you have something that David no longer has—the possibility of your life getting better, the possibility of finding hope again. The possibility of feeling loved in your life. And the possibility of recovering. Hold on to that."

The man whose stone read Gratitude said, "I want to thank you for inspiring me today."

"It's not just me," I said. "It's David's story that I hope will bring meaning to your life. If you ever need inspiration, feel free to stop by and see David. Unfortunately, he'll always be here."

As they said goodbye that day, they each shook my hand with a kind of warmth that felt very different from the guarded handshakes they'd offered when they first arrived. That's the meaning I will continue to make of my son's addiction.

Part III

Meaning

CHAPTER TWELVE

More Love Than Pain

I don't think of all the misery, but of all the beauty that remains."

—Anne Frank

The common belief is that grief is all about pain. Anyone who has been in grief would certainly agree with that. But I believe there is more. There is love. Why do we believe that the pain we feel is about the absence of love? The love didn't die when the person we love died. It didn't disappear. It remains. The question is: How do we learn to remember that person with more love than pain? This is a question, not a mandate. I am the first to say that there is no getting around the pain. We have to go through it because it is an inevitable result of the separation we are experiencing. It's a brutal, forced separation.

The word "bereaved" has its origins in the Old English words *deprived of*, *seized*, and *robbed*. That is how it feels when your loved one has been taken from you—as excruciating as if your arm had been ripped from your body. You've been robbed of what is dearest to you. The pain you feel is proportionate to the love you had. The deeper you loved, the deeper the pain. But you will find that love exists on the other side of the pain. It's actually the other face *of* pain.

Going through the Pain

You can't heal what you can't feel. Most people are afraid of what I call the "gang of feelings." Gangs intimidate us. They lurk, waiting for you to crack open the door so they can break in. Picture this gang: its members are anger, sadness, numbness, yearning, shock, and a lot of other hurtful emotions. The fear is that once you open the door to the gang, it will rush in and overwhelm you and you'll never be able to free yourself of them. People in fear of this gang often say things like, "If I start crying, I'll never stop." But crying, just like everything else in this life, does end. If you can allow yourself to feel the pain in all of its depths and cry it out, you might feel very sad, but you would not be overwhelmed by it. Instead, that feeling will move through you and you will be done with it. I'm not saying that you'll never again feel pain over the death of your loved one. You will. But you gave that particular moment of pain its due. You didn't resist it and you won't have to keep reliving it.

However, that's not how it happens for most of us. We fear the gang of feelings because we never let ourselves experience the entire emotion. Instead, we have emotions about our emotions. We begin to feel sad, and then we feel guilty that we're sad, which snaps us out of the sadness before we feel it completely. Or we're angry and we judge our anger, so we move into self-recrimination. Or we're sad but we think we should feel grateful. And on and on.

I encourage people to stay with the first generation of emotions. Ignore the comments your mind is making about your feelings. Otherwise the pain remains intact. Understand that there is a gang, but it's the gang of half-felt emotions. If you're sad, you need to stay with the sadness and feel it fully. Marianne Williamson says if you have a hundred tears to cry, you can't stop at fifty. The secret to remembering with love begins with accepting the pain, not trying to deny it or ignore it.

The Spiritual vs. the Human

There is a delicate balance that exists between what I think of as our immediate, human experience of loss and our spiritual experience of it. For many, our religious beliefs and our feeling of connection to God, or to some transcendent spiritual realm, can help get us through some of the toughest times. But no matter how deeply religious or spiritual we are, sometimes we want to be left in the humanness of our pain. There will be times when a grieving person does not want to be told that their loved one has gone to a better place or has gotten their heavenly reward or is with Jesus. For some people such words may be comforting whenever they are spoken. For others, never. And for still others, only at the right moment. After my son's death, a good friend asked me, "Whenever you're talking about your loss, do you want the spiritual response, human response, or both?" I thought it was great that she knew how to make that distinction.

When I talk about what to say to a grieving person, I tell people to notice if the griever is asking for you to see their human pain or their spiritual pain. All too often, rather than seeing them where they are, we give them a spiritual response, something we offer automatically without any awareness of the feelings of the bereaved. Sometimes we can be so heavenly minded we're no earthly good.

Every time I describe that resentment to the audiences at my lectures, I always get lots of nods of agreement. What people who have been through loss hear in such assurances is that they don't have to be in pain. But that's simply not true. Those of us who have lost someone dear *do* need to be in pain. I believe that my son, my parents, and everyone else I have loved who has died do continue on in the spiritual plane. But that doesn't mean I shouldn't miss them at the dinner table or yearn for one hug from them.

I understand that our friends and family want us not to be in pain, that it hurts them to see us that way. But sometimes when I would hear somebody say, "Your son is still with you in spirit," I wanted to say, "If I felt that instead of the pain, would you be more comfortable?" I didn't say it because I knew they meant well. They simply didn't understand where I was in the process of grief. Admittedly, it's very hard to know what's going on in someone else's mind. But if I'm asked my advice on this subject, I always suggest erring on the side of restraint and using the human response. Unless you feel very confident that a religious or spiritual reassurance will be well received, don't offer it first.

Facing the Storm

Jasmine sat on a pillow on the floor at the front of the room during one of my retreats. She was quiet and withdrawn. All I knew about her was that she had a child that died. Toward the end of the weekend, I asked people what was hardest for them. She raised her hand. It was the first time she had participated in any way, so I called on her, curious about what she would say.

"People keep telling me I can have another child, and that I should take comfort in that," she said.

"As if your child was replaceable?" I said.

"Yes, as if this one doesn't matter because I'll have another one soon."

"How long has it been since your child died?"

She froze as if she couldn't utter the words. I walked over and knelt beside her and said, "You're not alone."

She started rocking from side to side as if the truth was too much to bear. Then she said, "Five weeks."

"Oh, honey," I said. "At five weeks there is nothing *but* pain. The people who are telling you that you can have another child mean well. They can't stand for you to be in such terrible pain. But they can't take that pain away from you, and neither can I. For now, all I can do is be with you and let you know that during this weekend, we're all walking next to you."

"How long has it been?" is one of the first questions I always ask. It's not because there is some invisible timeline to grief. "How long has it been?" is my way of asking, "How much time have you had to process the pain?" I was struck by Jasmine's courage to come to a grief retreat only five weeks in. Later, when I asked her how she had found the strength to show up, she said, "I needed a place where I could be in deep despair without people trying to help me get over it."

Her instincts were correct. In five weeks after a loved one dies, there is no finding a way around the pain, no "getting over it." Feeling that pain is a necessary part of remembering the love. The pain is a part of the love. We can't love someone and lose them without feeling pain. Not only do we have a need to feel the pain, we also need to have it witnessed by others, not pushed away.

It's not just our friends and family who want to keep us from pain. Sometimes the bereaved want to push it away, too. I understand why some people are tempted to try to avoid it. When they sense that gang of feelings waiting to carry them off, they'll do anything they can think of to keep it at bay. One way to do that is to keep busy, to find ways to distract themselves.

My friend's twenty-three-year-old brother, with whom she was very close, died during the summer. She was a workaholic before his death and she continued working nonstop after his death. I wondered how she would do during the Christmas holidays when her family was planning to be together. This had been their tradition for many years. "I bet the holidays are going to be hard this year without your brother," I said.

"I've planned a million things for the kids and the family," she told me. "We're going to be too busy to be unhappy."

I hoped that would work, but my experience tells me that grief may get postponed, but it cannot be eradicated. Besides throwing yourself into an endless round of activities, there are many other ways of going numb to avoid the pain of grief, including drugs, alcohol, and sex. If you feel the artificial high, you don't have to feel the deep pain of grief—at least not during the temporary high.

Shopping is another way to stuff our feelings. A thirty-eight-year-old woman I know whose husband died went out and bought a Corvette. She had always dreamed of having one. "It seemed like it made perfect sense at the time," she said. "Somehow I thought that throwing a Corvette at the grief might retard its growth. It was like throwing a glass of water on a house fire."

One night I happened to come upon a documentary called *Facing the Storm*, about the buffalos in Montana. Robert Thomson of the Montana Department of Fish, Wildlife and Parks discussed how buffalo run into the storm, thus minimizing how long they will be in it. They don't ignore it, run from it, or just hope it will go away, which is what we often do when we want to avoid our storms of emotion. We don't realize that by doing this we're maximizing our time in the pain. The avoidance of grief will only prolong the pain of grief. Better to turn toward it and allow it to run its natural course, knowing that the pain will eventually pass, that one of these days we will find the love on the other side of pain.

Moving into the Love

When is it time to move into the love? When you feel that you have fully felt the pain. Even when you do, it will hurt again. It will just hurt less, and less often. Moving into love begins with realizing the love was always there. It was there in the good times, in the illness, in the death, and in the grief. It was never absent, even in the worst moments, and it is there still. Death is not strong enough to end love.

People whose loved ones died terrible deaths will sometimes object by saying, "Love wasn't there when he was murdered, or when she died alone, or when they went down in that plane."

My response is, "I don't believe that you stopped loving them in that moment."

"No, but my loved one didn't feel it."

How do you know? We are made up of love. We are the sum total of love. If I've felt one moment of real love in my life, that can be with me in my most terrifying moments. Love is a cushion in our tragedies. Love never dies. In our darkest moments, love remains. When everything else is gone, love continues.

Ron remembers how much his wife, Faith, suffered during her illness. But he also recalls how loved she was, and how much that meant to her.

We didn't think Faith would survive the cancer. I believe the chemo she did gave her more time. When I look back on the love, I think that played a role, too. What I remember most during her first hospitalization was when two of her friends came in and decorated Faith's room. They didn't bring her flowers. Instead, because they knew that art was her great love, they put up photos and posters of great masterpieces on every single wall. There was even a print of the *Mona Lisa*. In those dark days when she was violently ill and throwing up from the chemo, she would ask Mona Lisa if she had ever been this sick.

We owned a small art gallery and had only one employee. We loved running it together. But after Faith got sick she was so weak and spent so much time in the hospital that she was rarely able to come back to work. Since I had to go to the gallery most days, I got our friends and family together and came up with a schedule so she wouldn't be alone too much even if I couldn't be with her. There was never a day she went without visitors. Someone always brought her lunch and I usually brought dinner.

There were three hospitalizations, and with each one the staff would joke that Faith brought her decorators with her. During the last hospitalization, not long before she died, a nurse remarked how wonderful it was to be surrounded by art. Faith corrected her and said, "It's not art. It's love." She told the nurse that every poster, photo, wall decoration, and even the food people brought that she couldn't eat were all love.

There was no getting around the fact that what she was going through was awful—the chemo, the nausea, and the terror of dying. But symbolically, her friends were saying, "While you're in pain, we can remind you of our love." I see that love was her constant companion in pain. Now that Faith is gone, I've been surrounded by that same love. Faith was so young and I miss her every day, but I'm so grateful for the love.

One of my art clients had visited Faith in the hospital where he saw the art her friends had put on the walls. He thought it strange they would spend so much time decorating a hospital room, making it beautiful, even though everything would be taken down as soon as Faith left. He didn't see the point. After she died he said to me, "All that energy that went into putting the art on those walls was for naught. It didn't save her."

I don't know why he thought that. It mattered to her and it mattered to us. I can only hope when my time comes, I'll be surrounded by such love.

Paying attention to the love means simply noticing it. Faith was able to see, even in her worst moments, that love was present. That helped her to see to the other side of pain. And Ron, in turn, has been able to see to the other side of his pain. There are a million sayings that acknowledge the truth of this, such as *What we appreciate, appreciates.* However, it may require a very proactive mind to do that appreciating, especially in times of sorrow and pain.

Psychologist Rick Hanson says, "The brain is very good at learning from bad experiences, yet very, very bad at learning from good experiences. Neuroprocessing is privileged for negative stimuli. When a bad thing happens, we give more attention to the negative." He describes our minds as Velcro for the bad experiences (everything sticks), and Teflon for the good (nothing sticks).

We are wired to *not* smell the roses—like Ron's client. Negative moments, which are held in both short-term and long-term memory, become deeply wired and burned into our psyche. The same is not true for the positive ones, which are less likely to make it into the long-term memory bank. This is why you might quickly forget many of the wonderful moments with your loved one, but the negative ones will live on in endless repetition. It's thought that our minds are wired this way because of the survival benefits it offers: "Survival requires urgent attention to possible bad outcomes but less urgent [attention] with regard to good ones," according to Roy F. Baumeister, a professor of social psychology at Florida State University, who wrote about this in a journal article he coauthored, "Bad Is Stronger Than Good," which appeared in *The Review of General Psychology.*

Since our minds are wired for the negative, how do we find love through all that pain? Rick Hanson teaches a technique that has been widely used, called "Installing the good" or sometimes "Taking in the good." It helps us to find ways to give more attention to the good. I use the following technique to help people remember *all the moments* of their lives with their loved ones who died.

THE THREE STEPS OF TAKING IN THE GOOD

1. Identify a positive experience or memory. Hanson gives the example of thinking how good your coffee tasted this morning. You can do this with any positive experience, from the most ordinary to the most meaningful. In terms of the person who died, think about a wonderful moment you shared. It doesn't have to be anything extraordinary, just something that made you both happy. Maybe you watched a sunset together, read a poem to each other, took a two-hour walk through a city you loved. As Emily in the play *Our Town* was advised, when she was given the chance to return to earth for any day of her choosing, "Pick the least important day in your life. It will be important enough." Remember it in as much detail as you can—what you were both wearing, what the weather was like, what you said to each other, any sounds or smells or sensations associated with it.

2. Enrich it. Savor it. Think about it. Repeat it over and over in your mind. Sustain the memory of that good time for twenty to thirty seconds. Recapture the feeling of it in your body and emotions. Intensify it.
3. Absorb the experience. Sink into it and let it sink into you. Soak it in. Feel it in your body, visualize it in your mind, let it become part of you.

Learning to live with loss is like any other kind of learning. And learning to find the good even as we are in pain is a particularly difficult kind of learning. We can't learn with platitudes (e.g., "Be grateful for the time you had together"). But I think this technique can help integrate the good with the bad. I want grieving people to see the relevance in all that has happened. There is pain in their loss, but there is also good. I want to help them savor the love, not just stay with the pain. I want to help them find meaning in their memories and take that good into their future. If you see only the pain in a situation, it will grow. I'm not suggesting you minimize or negate it, but if that's all you pay attention to, that's all you'll have.

Don't Forget the Middle

Pain is never the whole story. We may get lost in it for a while, but there's always something more. Four years after his father died of a brain tumor at the age of forty-five, Mike was still overwhelmed by the pain of having watched his father's last days. His father, Jackson, had been a college football coach, a very strong and physically active man, and Mike often talked about how hard it had been to see his once powerful dad reduced to a shell of a man. Mike was stuck, unable to move past the memory of his father as sick and weak, continually replaying in his mind images of his father's suffering at the end.

But something shifted for him one Thanksgiving. That year

the whole family gathered for Thanksgiving, as it always did, and it didn't take long for Mike to start talking once again about how horrible it had been to see his dad so frail. He said to his uncle, Ralph, his father's brother:

"Do you remember that last Thanksgiving? He couldn't eat. Dad could barely walk. I think about that poor man all the time."

His uncle said to him, "Come, let's take a walk."

Mike followed Ralph outside. When they got to the sidewalk, Ralph stopped and began scrolling through something on his phone.

"What's happening?" Mike asked.

"Hang on," Ralph said. "There's something I want you to hear."

Mike stood there, not sure what his uncle was looking for.

"Here it is," Ralph said after a minute or two, and then played a voice mail message he had saved from Mike's dad.

"Hey, Ralph, thanks for coming in for my birthday yesterday. It meant a lot."

Mike leaned into the phone as if to get closer to his dad. The message continued.

"I had the best time playing football with you, Mike, and the neighbors. Mike and I are about to go on a hike. I couldn't think of a better way to spend my birthday. Thanks again!"

Mike paused to take it in and said, "Wow, I forgot about that day."

"I could see that you did. That's why I played this. The end of your dad's life was horrible. We'll never forget that. But I don't want you to forget the middle. He was a strong happy man for most of his life. He had a lot of wonderful days. You need to remember those days, too."

For Mike, who had been so lost in his pain for so long, that was a real eye-opener. Being able to remember his father as a happy man and a loving father helped him move, finally, past the pain that had been tormenting him into love for the father who had so clearly treasured his time with his son.

Love Bursts

When we move through pain and we release it, we fear there will be nothing, but the truth is, when the pain is gone, we are connected *only in love*. Though much of my work is about giving people permission to grieve fully after a loss, I also want to give them permission to keep loving. When I talk about remembering my son with love instead of pain, I recognize that love didn't stop with his death. His body died but the love didn't. Look for the small seeds of love in the pain. Just like a delicate plant, we have to pay attention to it and nourish it. If we do, the love will flower once again in our hearts.

I often talk about grief bursts. Even though someone may think they've put the worst of their grief behind them, they have moments when, seemingly out of the blue, they burst into tears, overwhelmed with feelings of loss. These moments are all the more painful because they are so unexpected, and people are often caught off balance by them. But there are comparable experiences that I call love bursts—those moments when suddenly, for no reason at all, we feel a surge of emotion for someone and tell them how much we love them. Contrary to what you might expect, those moments don't end with death. There will be times when you will suddenly well up with love for the person you lost. You may feel that that love has nowhere to go because you can't hold your loved one, but the love continues. If you allow yourself to feel it, you will find great meaning.

People in grief identify with my descriptions of both love bursts and grief bursts. When they hear the names I've given them, they are relieved to know that these experiences are common enough among the bereaved to *warrant* names. It validates their experience and lets them know that what they're feeling is normal. When people tell me they're dealing with overwhelming emotions, I've learned to ask them, "Is this a grief burst or a love burst?" This is one more way I help them pay attention to the love.

Sometimes I encourage people who are trying to comfort a bereaved person to ask about a favorite memory. Or to share one of their own. "I was just thinking about your mother's smile the other day," they might say. "What joy she brought to all of us!" Or "Your son gave the best hugs." Or "Going places with your husband was always so much fun because he made everyone laugh, even the person in the ticket booth at the movie theater and the waitress in the coffee shop."

Don't be afraid that these memories will bring pain. They are deep sources of comfort to those who are in mourning. How often do we talk about regrets and forget to remember all the good we felt in the relationship? Many of us can remember only the negatives. Be sure to remember the love.

CHAPTER THIRTEEN

Legacy

Strange, isn't it? Each man's life touches so many
other lives. When he isn't around he leaves an awful
hole, doesn't he?

—*It's a Wonderful Life*

When we think about legacies—what is left behind after someone dies—there are many kinds. First there are the legacies that
the individual person leaves. These can be large public legacies
like major donations to museums and hospitals, universities
and foundations, or maybe rooms or entire buildings that bear
her name.

In 2010, Bill and Melinda Gates and Warren Buffett created
the Giving Pledge, a campaign to encourage billionaires to commit to donating half or more of their wealth to philanthropic
causes during their lifetime. By 2018, nearly two hundred people, including Michael Bloomberg, George Kaiser, Mark Zuck-
erberg, and George Lucas had signed on to the Giving Pledge.

This kind of generosity is not confined to billionaires. In
fact, the founders of the Giving Pledge say that it was inspired
by the example of millions of people at all income levels who
give—often at great personal sacrifice—to make the world a
better place. Perhaps your loved one funded a scholarship, and
now every year, twenty students will be the beneficiaries of her
generosity. They are part of her legacy. Or perhaps she just volunteered at a soup kitchen or brought food and clothing to the
homeless person who lived on her corner.

Chances are she also left behind friends and family members who are better off for having known her. This is the kind of legacy that anyone, rich or poor, can bequeath. Each of us affects many people throughout our lives. The movie *It's a Wonderful Life* does a brilliant job of helping us realize how many people we affect in our lives without realizing it. It tells the story of George Bailey, who at a moment of crisis comes to believe that the world would be a better place if he had never lived, and is about to throw himself off a bridge. Through a divine or a semidivine intervention (it's not an angel who helps him but rather an angel-in-training), he is prevented from killing himself and allowed to see the ways in which his family and his community would have been worse off had he not been a part of their lives. Through various acts of vigilance, kindness, generosity, self-sacrifice, and love, he had saved his younger brother's life; prevented his boss, a pharmacist, from accidentally poisoning a child by giving him the wrong medicine; averted the bankruptcy of the town savings and loan where everyone had deposited their savings by shoring it up with his own hard-earned money; and married a woman who adored him, with whom he fathered two loving children. The film shows us that legacies are a mixture of who we are and what we have done. It was true for George Bailey and it's true for your loved one who died.

When I think about my father's legacy, I remember that he was a dreamer. He never thought about whether something was possible or not. If I told my father that I wanted to be an astronaut, his response was, "What's your rocket going to look like?" He never said, "You have to become a pilot first," or, "NASA accepts very few people." Part of his legacy is that he gave me enormous confidence to tackle anything.

And then there was Steve Jobs. When Steve Jobs died, some people put Post-it notes on Apple store windows thanking him. Some said, "Thanks for my iPhone, iPad, iPod, or Mac." But the majority of the messages were about learning to think differently because of him. His brand wasn't actually Apple.

Apple was the by-product. His brand was thinking differently. The people who remember his legacy will enhance their lives by thinking differently.

What We Do Honors Our Loved Ones

We can honor our loved one in the form of foundations and donations, buildings with their names on them, scholarships in their honor, or much more modest forms.

My nephew Jeffrey loved to go on walks in Central Park with his wife, daughter, and their dog. He noticed things the rest of the world often overlooked. While most people saw a bench in Central Park as a place to sit, Jeffrey noticed they had small plaques on them. "Each of these benches represents a story about a person," he would remark, and he loved reading those little stories, which said things like: "I love you very much and look forward to marrying you ... but if we have a fight you can always sleep here"; "After standing by me through thick and thin for 45 years, have a seat"; and "In loving memory of Tille Goldman. She loved New York in June. She loved a Gershwin tune. Central Park was her estate for 95 wonderful years (1906–2001)."

Now Jeffrey is one of those stories, because when he died, his wife bought a bench for him. It says: "For Jeffrey B. Hodes (1964–2011), who adored this city and park. May his spirit soar here."

Liz and Steve Alderman from New York turned their pain into purpose in order to leave a legacy for their son Peter. He was twenty-five years old when he died on September 11, 2001, while attending a conference at Windows on the World, a restaurant on the 107th floor of the World Trade Center's north tower.

Liz said, "I always felt that if a child of mine was ever killed, I would never be able to stop screaming. But you can't keep screaming. I realized you only have two choices: You either kill yourself—crawl into bed and never get out—or you put one foot in front of the other." She says she is not the same person she used to be and that's okay.

The Aldermans knew they wanted to do something to honor Peter. They just weren't sure what. Then one night, Liz saw an ABC *Nightline* program called "Invisible Wounds," featuring Dr. Richard Mollica, a Harvard expert on traumatized populations.

"I learned that there were one billion people who had directly experienced torture, terrorism, and mass violence around the globe—one-sixth of humanity—and 50 to 70 percent had such traumatic depression they could no longer lead functional lives," Liz said.

Ten days later, the Aldermans had a meeting in Mollica's office that led to the launch of the Peter C. Alderman Foundation in 2002. It works to heal the victims of terrorism and mass violence by training indigenous health workers and establishing clinics around the globe. It currently funds eight facilities: two in Cambodia, four in Uganda, one in Liberia, and one in Kenya, treating thousands of patients. Peter died as a victim of terrorism and nothing can undo that, but there are millions of people who have experienced terrorism, torture, violence, and trauma who can't lead functional lives.

Liz said, "If we can return some of these people to life in Peter's name, there is no better memorial for Pete than that. It is a mark that he lived." She continues: "Peter didn't have the opportunity to make the world a better place," said Liz. "My loss is horrendous, but his is worse. He never got to live his life. I thought I'd never feel good about anything after he was killed, but I feel good about this work."

Peter's father gave sound advice when he said, "If you want to feel better, go help someone. You don't have to help a lot of people. Just do it once. You'll see. You'll do it again."

You don't have to have money to create a legacy for your loved ones. Another bereaved parent who took action in memory of his son was Dadarao Bilhore, a vegetable stall vendor in

Mumbai, India. I read about him after noticing a headline in the *LA Times* that said, "Father Finds Solace in Filling Up Potholes After Son's Death." Based on a story originally reported by Yahoo News India, it described how Dadarao Bilhore began filling up potholes and smoothing road surfaces every day in honor of his late son, Prakash, who had died at sixteen from a road accident caused by potholes. For Bilhore, filling the potholes, which he hopes will prevent future accidents and spare other parents the pain of losing a child, has helped him deal with the death of his son. "Wherever I go," he said about his work, "I feel Prakash is standing with me." Three years after Prakash's death, his father had filled in nearly six hundred potholes in the notoriously shoddy roads of Mumbai.

The bereaved can do so many things to honor their loved ones' legacies. Foundations and endowed scholarships and buildings named after their loved ones are of course wonderful. But they can also write down their memories in a memory book to share with friends and family. They can continue to observe traditions and visit places that were meaningful to that person. They can help take care of children or other family members or pets the person left behind. They can volunteer or march on behalf of a cause that the loved one believed in. The list is endless.

A Legacy of Remembering

We often say how much we miss our loved ones but we don't always realize that missing them is part of remembering them, and how you remember your loved one is part of their legacy. I was touched by the movie *Coco*, a lovely animated children's film about the afterlife. It tells the story of young Miguel's adventures in the Land of the Dead during the Day of the Dead, the holiday that Mexicans observe every year in honor of the loved ones they have lost. Miguel learns that remembering and celebrating the dead is an important tradition because it keeps us in touch with the spirits of the deceased. As long as someone still cares enough to remember them, the dead get to keep "living" in a society that is not so different from the one they left behind. Once they are forgotten in the living world, they disappear.

My generation mourned the death of one of our most beloved actresses, Carrie Fisher, who was best known for her *Star Wars* movies. I met her when she called me because a friend of hers was dying and she was bringing him to her home. She wanted my help in making sure he had a sweet, peaceful death. When I arrived at her home, it was filled with colorful items of her life, and also from our pop culture, such as a Princess Leia doll. I explained that inviting a dying friend into your home for his final days is no small thing. She said she understood, but she wanted to help him and be there for him. That kindness will always be part of what I remember as her legacy.

I think of Carrie often as she and my son are in the same cemetery in Los Angeles. Her legacy was continued by her daughter, Billie Lourd. She found her own unique way to honor her mother. On the first anniversary of Fisher's death, Lourd created a poetic tribute to her late mother, which she posted on Instagram:

> Momby had an otherworldly obsession with the northern lights, but I never got to see them with her. We journeyed to northern Norway to see if we might "see the heavens lift up her dark skirts and flash her dazzling privates across [our] unworthy irises." And she did. I love you times infinity.

Visiting a place that was special to our loved ones helps us remember and connects us to their legacies. It doesn't have to be anywhere special. It just has to have been important to them. Sometimes walking in their footsteps is all you need to do to find a legacy of gratitude for having known them.

We Are Their Legacy

You can honor your loved ones by seeing how they have changed you. This involves finding a connection with that person that you can carry forward into your own life. Bonnie MacBird, a friend of mine who writes Sherlock Holmes novels, told me how she continues her father's legacy.

When I complimented the food she served at dinner one night, she said, "I'm a horrible cook. I just follow recipes. I'm so insecure about my cooking. My father was an amazing cook. I try to embody him when I cook."

I remarked that that was a sweet legacy. "Do you have any other legacies around him?"

She smiled and said, "Absolutely! He had one arm partially amputated and had a hook for an arm and hand. But after you were with him for a few minutes, you forgot about it. He didn't carry himself like someone who was physically challenged. When some people lose a limb, it becomes their calling card. Those few become what they lost. I'm sure my father dealt with the sadness when it happened, but it never became his identity. In fact, he built an addition to our house when I was growing up. Now that he's gone, whenever I start to feel like something is unfair, when I feel wronged or overwhelmed, I think of him and how he dealt with his hardship. If my dad could add a room onto our house with one arm, I can do whatever is in front of me."

Ensuring that the good qualities of your loved one will live on in your own life is perhaps the most meaningful of all legacies. Something Billie Lourd was quoted as saying after her mother's death embodies that: "Finding the funny might take awhile, but I learned from the best, and her voice will forever be in my head and in my heart."

If on the other hand the person you lost left behind a predominantly negative legacy, you can sometimes reshape that legacy into something more positive, creating meaning from darkness. The story of what happened after the death of billionaire J. Paul Getty is an example of all the different facets of legacy.

Despite the fact that he had the largest fortune in the world, Getty always felt poor. This was a rich man who put a phone booth in his private residence, so he wouldn't have to pay for other people's phone calls. He would spend millions on a piece of art that he hoarded and never showed to anyone. He was best known to the world for a stinginess so extreme that he was not even willing to pay a ransom for his grandson, J. Paul Getty III, when he was kidnapped—until the kidnappers sent an ear they had cut from the grandson's head and a note saying that they would be delivering the rest of him, piece by piece, until the ransom was paid. That horrifying, very well-publicized episode would have been his legacy had his family, after his death, not chosen to reshape it by creating a trust. The J. Paul Getty Trust is the world's largest cultural and philanthropic organization dedicated to the visual arts. It comprises world-class museums, where admission is free, a research institute, and a conservation institute.

You can honor a person's legacy in how you grieve. You are the living demonstration of grief to your children. Will they be able to say something like, "I remember how she took us to Dad's grave and she cried openly in front of us"? Or "She talked about what a wonderful man he was and encouraged us to share our memories of him." Or "She taught us that life would go on after he died."

Or will they remember that you withdrew from them, that you never spoke of their father again and didn't allow them to, and you became bitter and cold. This is part of the legacy that you'll be leaving for your children and the people around you. We grieve as a tribe and we're always modeling for that tribe.

Earlier in the book, I talked about husbands and wives who felt they had to stop living after their spouse had died as a sign of loyalty. I counseled them to understand that was not something their loved one would have wanted. But it isn't only romantic partners who find it difficult to live well after loss. Many other people do, too.

I once worked with a woman who told me her twin sister had died three years earlier and her life had felt empty ever since. "We were together for forty-five years," Martha said in tears. "I hear people talk about how hard it is for someone to lose a spouse after forty-five years. They seem to understand how painful that would be. But people who are married had a life before they met each other. I've never been in the world without my twin sister. Now that she's gone, I can't find purpose or meaning in life anymore."

Grief was engulfing her. She cycled through Kübler-Ross's stages over and over again, read books, and did everything she could think of to help herself, but nothing made it any better.

"Who's in your life now?" I asked her.

"I have my husband and my two twin girls."

"Wow," I said, "twins run in your family. So you have two legacies to deal with, your sister's for you, and yours for your daughters. Think of them as two separate jobs, to grieve and to love."

"I have the first one down," she shot back. "I'm grieving all the time."

"Okay," I said. "Let's talk about the loving, because it relates to grieving. Can you tell me a happy moment from your childhood that you shared with your sister and your mother?"

She smiled and said, "Dessert. We got to taste desserts before they were baked. Mom always made desserts for Sunday dinner and we'd help her cook. It was so much fun for us to cook with her."

"That does sound like fun," I said. "Do you have another sweet memory of you, your sister, and your mom?"

"Absolutely. Mom would sing to us at bedtime. Her songs made us feel safe."

"If you have two, I bet you have hundreds."

"I do."

"How important are these memories?"

"They're everything. They made life special and I cherished them. I feel robbed now that my sister is gone and I can't share them with her anymore."

"Did your mom lose anyone she loved when you were growing up?"

Yes," she said. "I remember how she cried and cried when my grandmother died."

"Did all your sweet and funny moments with your mother end after that?"

"No."

"That's right, because your mother grieved and then she continued living and loving you. You have to do the same for your two daughters. As you said, you have the grieving part down. It's the living and loving you need to work on."

"How am I going to do that?" she asked.

"By looking at the people dearest to you. How are your twin girls doing? What sweet, funny memories are you creating for them? How are you making their childhoods special like your mom did for you? What cushion are you giving them to get through life?"

"That's a lightbulb," she said. "I never thought about trying to give them the same kind of wonderful memories that my mother gave me."

In that moment, Martha began to realize the legacies of both her mother and her sister. Her mother left her a legacy of happy moments that she and her sister had shared growing up. Her sister had left her a legacy of wonderful memories. But she hadn't thought about the legacy she was creating for her two daughters. She wouldn't want them to remember their aunt as someone who had turned their mother into someone who could no longer enjoy life or help them enjoy theirs. And she herself wouldn't want to be remembered that way. It would be better to create a legacy for her daughters that allowed them to see they could grieve for someone they love, and then go on to live.

The Legacy of Things

This is a place for a little more practical advice. The items a loved one left behind are part of their legacies. They are deeply meaningful because of whom they belonged to and the memories they call up. Which is why we may find it very difficult to part with any of them. Everything our loved ones touched—from their clothes to their jewelry, their house and everything in it, their car, their music collection, their books and their art—is the physical evidence of how our loved ones lived their lives, what they enjoyed, how they spent their time, what they valued, and what they found beautiful and meaningful.

Family members are often challenged by wanting to keep everything, which is usually impossible or impractical. But getting rid of things, whether by passing them on to family and friends or donating them or simply throwing them away, feels like we are being asked to shrink the evidence that they lived. Even taking practical steps like closing their bank and credit card accounts and having their phones turned off seems to make their footprint here on earth smaller. It was brutal enough to have to part with our loved ones and now we have to let go of their things, too? It seems too hard. I understand this feeling very well because I had many of the same issues when I had to dispose of my son's things.

Ultimately, however, our belongings can become a trap when we find ourselves unable to part with them. I often hear people say in my lectures, "I'm struggling. I can't let go of even the smallest things." What I have learned from my work is that as we decrease the outer evidence that our loved ones lived, we must increase the evidence inside of us.

I help people understand that they themselves are the biggest piece of evidence of their loved ones' lives. You are unique in all the world for having known that person. You are the living, breathing evidence that the person lived. I have my father's watch, but it's the memories of him that live inside of me that matter more than the watch. I am the keeper of those memories, I can share stories of him as a father, the many funny, tender moments we shared. Who I am is very much a product of who he was. In that way I am the most important part of what my father has left on this earth. So while we may have to let go of someone's belongings, the person himself will forever live in us, and in our memories. And the belongings may find surprising, meaningful afterlives, too.

Joanne Carson, a television personality and former wife of Johnny Carson, reached out to me through a mutual friend. She had survived a lot of loss in her life and now her own health was declining. We had many conversations during her last few years. One afternoon she brought me into a room in her house where Truman Capote had done a lot of his writing—and where he died.

Joanne and Truman had been good friends and they had always had a tender spot for one another. She told me something about the life battles, both physical and mental, that he had fought. Sitting down, with great gentleness on the bed in the room, she told me, with tears in her eyes, "This is where I held Truman as he died. I told him it was okay to go."

Today I'm writing this chapter on Truman Capote's desk. To some people, it's just a desk. But since I know its history, it has great meaning for me. Part of the meaning is through Joanne. Looking at it, I feel her love for him, another part of the meaning is being able to feel connected in some small way to a great writer. As I sit at his desk writing my own book, I can only wonder what he wrote here. Which books? Which letters? While I'm writing about grief and healing, he wrote about murders that caused terrible grief and suffering to people, even as he was battling his own demons. What pain might he have been feeling, here at this desk?

I also think about how fortunate he was to have had a friend who saw the "wounded child" in him—someone I would later be able to call a friend, too. This desk was one of many things Truman Capote bequeathed her, most of which she eventually

sold at an auction—"The Private World of Truman Capote"—
which was a very high-profile event. An animal lover, Joanne
donated part of the proceeds of the auction to pet-related char-
ities. That was her way of making meaning out of the physical
objects of her friend's life.

As you think about how to do something meaningful with
the things that are in *your* possession, I encourage you to photograph the things you care about before letting them go. I've
found that you can get the same emotional reaction from a
photo as you do from the item itself. I don't have to keep my
father's Mercury Comet station wagon to remember how much
pleasure he got from it. I can get the same feeling from looking at a picture of my father waving at us from the driver's seat
with a big smile on his face. If I have a picture of Dad in his
suit, I don't actually have to keep the suit.

Then I suggest you choose the possessions that mean the
most to you and dispose of the rest. It can be helpful to have
someone with you when you sort through things, because they
can be much more objective about what to hold on to than you
are. Some things you may want to share with family members
and friends who also loved the person. A ring that belonged
to your mother might mean the world to her sister. Your son
may be thrilled to have your husband's watch. The beautiful
rug your father bought when he was in Morocco might bring
back happy memories to his best friend who used to stay with
him whenever he visited. The family dining table where you all
gathered for festive meals may bring joy to your daughter.

Sometimes when people tell me they are having trouble letting go of their loved ones' possessions, I try to help them find
ways to bring continued meaning to these possessions, even
as they are saying goodbye to them. They might bring them in
so we can talk about them before they give them away. Sharing them with me is sharing a part of their loved ones. I might
explain that they're not just getting rid of their father's suit. It's
going to someone who needs a job so he can give his family a
better life. Or they're not losing their husband's watch. They'll

be seeing it on their son's wrist for years to come. All of these things can become part of a legacy that continues to serve and give pleasure to others long after your loved one is gone.

Living On Online

One challenge that has arisen only in recent years is what to do about your loved ones' online legacies. Large parts of our lives are now spent online, and our deaths will make their way online one way or another, too. Figuring out how to handle social media after a death is a process that is still evolving.

Denise found out the hard way that this can be fraught with problems. She said, "My brother had a social media account that was very active. I knew that I would have to decide whether to keep it going or to turn it into a memorial page that clearly acknowledged his death. Turning it into a memorial page felt like one more finality."

Social media is grappling with what happens to our pages after we die and how these digital remembrances and tombstones will be viewed. A friend told me that after her mother died, she uploaded all the family portraits to her social media. She wanted it to be not be only a legacy but a history for her grandkids. Before she memorialized the social media page, she added all her photos, so it became a living, breathing photo album dedicated to her mother's life.

Think of this work as another way of building someone's legacy. Along with everything else you are doing—writing an obituary and/or eulogy, sorting through his possessions, revisiting the places he loved, talking to friends and family about him, sharing memories—you are shaping the way he will be remembered. You are also beginning the process of reconstructing your own life. Nothing will return you to the way you were before you lost your loved one. But everything you do to help his legacy to flourish and grow will help you grow, too. As I said earlier, your grief won't get smaller. But you will get bigger.

CHAPTER FOURTEEN

Grieving to Believing: The Afterlife

It is very beautiful over there.
—Thomas Edison's last words

Oh wow, oh wow, oh wow.
—Steve Jobs's last words

I often get called in by the authorities to help people in the most horrific situations. This particular call was about counseling the parents of a two-month-old baby, Ethan, who had been mauled to death by the family dogs. As I was on my way to their home, I wondered what I could possibly do to help them grieve the death of their child. When I got there, I sat on the floor with Jane, a woman in her midtwenties, who had just spent her first Mother's Day childless. She talked about how hard it was to comprehend it all. "I can't make sense of it," she said. "They were our family dogs. They've been around our son from the day he was born."

"I don't think anyone will ever be able to make sense of this," I said. "In this pain, have you found anything that has brought you a moment of peace or comfort since Ethan died?"

She gave me an animated, "Yes. Ethan is here with me, watching over me. I feel him all the time."

There was a time when that feeling of connection with Ethan would have been dismissed or viewed as some kind of unhealthy denial of reality. But now there is a body of work that views it in a positive way, acting like a life raft that can support us in a turbulent sea of pain.

These ideas about connection and continuity have been influenced by Dennis Klass, PhD, a professor at Webster University in St. Louis, Missouri, whose interest in death, dying, and bereavement work began in 1968 when he was a graduate assistant in Elisabeth Kübler-Ross's death and dying seminar at the University of Chicago. Since then, Klass has written extensively about what he calls the continuing bonds model of grief, which was first introduced in 1996 in a collection of essays by various psychologists, academics, nurses, and others that he coedited with Phyllis Silverman and Steven Nickman. The twenty or so experts who contributed to *Continuing Bonds* viewed the natural course of bereavement as a process not of relinquishing bonds with the dead but of retaining them and having our lives enriched by them.

As I heard Phyllis Silverman explain once, the concept was controversial at first. She recounted an exchange she'd had with a colleague at a bereavement conference who insisted that healthy grieving required you to put the past behind you and let go of your relationship with the person who died. Silverman disagreed. Having recently experienced the birth of a grandson, she said that just as birth is about a change in the mother's connection to the infant who was once inside of her, so is death a change in our relationship to the person who is no longer here but still lives within us. Death does not end a relationship, she insisted. It changes it. I agree, and from what I've seen of people who are in grief, they are much better off because of that continuing relationship.

And yet there are still psychologists and counselors who try to discourage such relationships. Cynthia, whose son died, told me that she had seen a counselor about her grief. The counselor advised her to find closure by writing a farewell letter to her son, ending the relationship. She was horrified and never went back to that person. Luckily, she listened to her gut and found out that it didn't resonate with other counselors, either.

One of the reasons Elisabeth Kübler-Ross and I wanted to formally adopt her stages from dying to grief was because so many people misunderstood them. They saw them as a map of a relationship that would end when they finally accepted the death of their loved one. But the five stages of grief were never meant to be an end unto themselves, and completion of them wasn't supposed to signify the ending of the relationship or grief. Kübler-Ross herself felt connected to people who had died and did not believe that death was an ending. I hope that by offering a sixth stage of grief, I can encourage people to understand how the continuing evolution of their relationship with the person who died will help them find their way to meaning.

The mother of a friend of mine died a few years ago from cancer. I never got to know John's mother when she was alive, but I feel like I know her now because John has a unique way of carrying her with him into the world. The same way you and I might say, "My friend Cindy would love this restaurant," John might say, "My mom loves this place." If you didn't know she was dead, you might just think she's in Kansas. This is how he chooses to keep her with him. She is ever present in his reality.

John is not in denial about his mother's death. He went through an intense period of grief and mourning after she died. But now that he has accepted that she is gone, treating his mother as if she is still here is how he finds a meaningful relationship with her in death.

When someone dies, the relationship doesn't die with them. You have to learn how to have a new relationship with them. You can still keep learning from them in your everyday life. An instant will come up and remind you of something that happened between you and your deceased loved one, and now that he or she is gone, you can see it from a different point of view. As I get older, I understand my mother better because I have now lived the same number of years—and more—that she did. I can see things from her side more than I ever could when she was alive, since I was too young to be able to do that then.

I carry my mother with me. She lives within me. When a subject comes up, I might say something about what I think she would have thought about it. I bring the past into the present. I feel that I am still learning from her, which helps me to go back and see the past differently. That is how our relationship continues to evolve and grow. That is how our relationship keeps gaining in meaning.

In our last book together, *On Grief and Grieving*, Elisabeth and I wrote that we didn't believe in the concept of closure after death. When we speak about grief, there are two closures that come to mind: The first is the unrealistic wrap-up we expect after a loss. It has become an added burden not just to mourn and grieve the loss, but to find that closure, and find it quickly, so you can move on.

The second kind of closure involves doing things that help put the loss in perspective, such as reviewing what happened and why—or looking for missing pieces of the stories and filling in the gaps. It can range from finding the killer of a loved one to finding a way to say goodbye after a loved one died at the end of a long struggle with illness.

You're not closing the door on a relationship with the person who died. You don't ever bring the grief over a loved one to a close. You're opening the door to a different relationship. Remaining connected to your loved one in grief is not "unhealthy grieving." It's normal. In death, our attachments continue, as does the love. Research regarding continuing bonds speaks to what I've seen in decades of work with bereaved people. Their connections continue to evolve. I recently asked people on my social media who had experienced a loss to tell me if they still had a relationship with the person who died. The answer was a resounding yes. Here are some of their comments.

"I feel my husband watching over me all the time. Taking care of me."

"My daughter died. I talk to her all the time, both out loud and in my head. I write to her as well. It helps me feel closer to her."

"I visit my son's grave and talk to him like he was still alive. I celebrate his birthday and his death. I felt that I lost part of myself when he left, but I also feel like he's with me. I loved him before he was born and I'm learning to love him after his death. Grief will never end. The pain will be with me until I die, but I find comfort by talking about him and thinking of our lives together."

"My mother's and my relationship has improved a great deal in the twenty years since she passed away. I think I've learned to understand her and look at her with more compassion."

"Dad has been gone for eight months and Mom has been gone for a year. It still feels like yesterday. I so miss them. But I talk to Mom and Dad all the time. I have wonderful dreams about them. I will love them forever."

"The relationship definitely continues with my loved one. I speak to Jake and feel he is with me constantly. My older son got married in Canada a month ago, and as I was walking down the aisle with my older son, I felt him following us. I felt it was our sweet Jake letting us know he was with us at his brother's wedding."

When I was visiting my son's grave recently, I went into the gift shop to grab some flowers. I like to bring David stones from places I visit, but still I bring flowers from time to time. I said to the woman behind the counter, "I guess flowers are your biggest seller here."

"Yes, they are," she said.

"What's your second-biggest seller?"

She pointed to the birthday section. It was filled with happy birthday signs, balloons, and other items that people put on their loved ones' graves to commemorate their birthdays. I found it moving to see that even birthday wishes would continue after death.

In some religious circles, there is a belief that if you have a connection with your deceased loved one, you are actually in communication with a demon in disguise. I'm not a religious expert, but after decades of watching the bereaved continuing their bonds with their loved ones, my feeling is that those bonds have something sacred about them. They are the very opposite of evil.

Eighty percent of bereaved people say that they have felt a loved one's presence at some point after they died. Many times, it occurs around one of our senses. You're riding on a train when out of the blue, you smell vanilla candles. But there are no candles—just a fragrance in the air that makes you feel the presence of your grandmother, who always had vanilla candles burning in her home. Perhaps you think you see your loved one walking in the middle of a crowd. Or you hear the voice of the person who died, speaking to you, giving you advice that turns out to be helpful. Or you're anxious about a meeting and you feel your husband's hand touch your shoulder reassuringly as you walk through the door. Or maybe there is just a general feeling that the person is in the room.

Do all those kinds of phenomena mean that there is an afterlife? This is a question I am often asked during my TV interviews. As I mentioned earlier, I believe in the concept of the afterlife. I think many people are comforted to hear a grief expert validate that idea. They see that they are not crazy and that it is normal to have these continuing connections. But I don't think that you have to believe in the existence of the afterlife to experience such connections.

Afterlife

I tell people up front that I speak many languages: Christian, evangelical Christian, Catholic, Jewish, atheist, agnostic, etc. In my work, I try to see people for who they are, and to meet them where they are. That means I have to be able to talk to them in their own language to help with their grief, and if that language does not include a belief in the afterlife, I avoid all talk about it. Though many people find great meaning and consolation in their religious beliefs about the afterlife, if there is no such belief, there will be no comfort in hearing someone talk about it. In fact, it is likely to annoy or even enrage them. And as I discussed earlier, even those who are believers may not want to hear that kind of attempt to comfort them. It may feel too much like a Hallmark card, something people just say when they don't really acknowledge the other person's pain. I have learned to be circumspect in what I say.

Years ago, I was talking with a colleague who teaches ethics at Loyola Marymount University. She was about to begin a class on death and dying, and as we were discussing end-of-life issues, I thought about all the patients I've worked with who have had visions on their deathbed, and all the discussions I've had over the years about these visions with my colleagues. At hospice, palliative-care, and other end-of-life conferences, such visions never get mentioned during the formal sessions. They would be considered too woo-woo for serious discussion. But after a long day of lectures, over a drink or two, people often start opening up about the patients who were behind the studies and reports they had presented earlier. One person might recount a patient's deathbed vision, and then another person tells a similar story, and suddenly the whole group falls into an animated discussion about who and what we see before we die and what, if anything, it means.

I decided to mention to this highly respected, well-credentialed professor a recent patient of mine who had had one of these visions. When I brought up the phenomenon of deathbed visions, I knew she would have a strong reaction one way or another. My guess was that she would dismiss it as unworthy of serious consideration. But she surprised me by having the opposite reaction. "It's so rarely written about," she said, "let alone discussed in a formal classroom setting. Everyone has these stories, but no one seems willing to put them down on paper."

Her words stayed with me, and after that conversation I was inspired to write a book called *Visions, Trips, and Crowded Rooms: Who and What You See Before You Die.* Based on interviews with physicians, psychiatrists, psychologists, social workers, nurses, priests, rabbis, and ministers, it discusses three unique phenomena encountered by many of the dying that challenge our ability to explain and fully understand the mystery of our final days.

The first phenomenon is "visions." As the dying lose sight of this world, some of them appear to be looking into the world to come.

The second experience is the feeling that they are getting ready to go on a "trip." During our loved ones' last hours, they may see their impending deaths as a transition or journey. These trips may seem to us to be all about leaving, but for the dying, they may be more about arriving. Mona Simpson, Steve Jobs's sister, said in the obituary she wrote for him that when she went to his deathbed, "His tone was affectionate, dear, loving, but like someone whose luggage was strapped onto the vehicle, who was already on the beginning of his journey, even as he was sorry, truly deeply sorry, to be leaving us."

The third phenomenon is "crowded rooms." The dying often repeat the word "crowded" over and over, as they talk about seeing many people filling the room where they await their death. They are people they have known in life who have died, as well as others we may not have known. Perhaps they were ancestors we never met in this life. In spiritual truth, we never die alone. In this world, we go to greet the new birth. What if there is another world where we go to greet the new death? Just as loving hands greeted us when we were born, so will loving arms embrace us when we die. In the tapestry of life and death, we may begin to see connections to the past that we missed in life. While death may look like a loss to the living, the last hours of a dying person may be full rather than empty.

Though the doctors and nurses and other people who are part of the health care establishment often bear witness to these phenomena among the dying, how do they interpret them? Are such phenomena accepted as legitimate and formally discussed and written about, or are they dismissed as dubious, borderline experiences? In their last moments on earth, how are the patients with deathbed visions viewed? Those outside of hospice and end-of-life services have long minimized and discounted the experiences of the dying. They attribute deathbed visions to pain medication, fever, or lack of oxygen to the brain. Discounting a patient's experience has probably been around as long as the dying have had visions. The sense of the dead coming to greet the dying has also been with us as long as people have experienced it. It offers the possibility that the afterlife is real, which is a comfort to those who are about to step into the great unknown.

When I think about my own beliefs about the afterlife, I come back to three possible options for how to look at it, and the meaning one can find in each of those three views.

> **Option one:** Your loved ones have died. They are in the afterlife and they have awareness of you. They see you grieving. They are aware of what's going on in your life. They continue to be in touch with this world. If this option is true, your loved ones have witnessed your pain and have seen how deeply you have grieved for them and how much you loved them. I believe that if that is the case, they would want to see you live again once some time has passed. I don't believe that your loved ones would be happy to see you stop living because they are gone. And if they are still aware of the physical world as you experience it, then I think you should want to show them a good time. When I went to Yosemite, I wanted my son to see it through my eyes because he never saw it when he was alive.
>
> **Option two:** Your loved ones are in the afterlife, but they are no longer in touch with this world. They have other things to do that we can't even begin to understand.

From your perspective, all you can do is grieve fully and then, in time, live fully.

Option three: This is the atheist view. Your loved ones died, and their consciousness became nothing. There may be some comfort in that, especially if your loved ones had difficult lives or suffered a lot during their final illness and death. But in terms of how to live after their death, we're back in the same place as with the other two options—that we should grieve fully, then live fully.

This brief ride we call life will be over soon enough for all of us. My son, my parents, and my nephew are gone from this life. Nothing is going to change that. I long to see them again and I will never be the same until I do. But when I do, I don't want to have to tell them that my life lost all its meaning when they died. They loved me, and they wouldn't want that.

I have seen the worst life has to offer. I've been to concentration camps. I've seen the World Trade Towers smoldering. I've consoled parents after school shootings, and I've met with victims of horror who were present when bombs went off at public events. I've sat with thousands of people in grief and they have all taught me that there is life after loss. After they have experienced their sorrow in all its fullness, they are able to find meaning and go on living and loving.

When people ask me if I believe in life after death for our loved ones and I tell them yes, I often turn the question around: "Do you believe there is life after death for us the living as well?" That is the question we must all answer. While we wish with all our hearts that we could have our loved ones back with us for even one more day, what about us? We were put on this earth for such a short time and we will never get to experience this life again. So why don't we think about how much one more day would mean in our own lives?

In the face of our great losses, life goes on. The world keeps spinning. The seasons change, the dead of winter gives way to the rebirth that occurs every spring. Every storm gives way to a clear new day. Despite our losses, we continue. We keep moving, taking in another breath. If we are still here when the new day dawns, it is an opportunity to explore the life that our loved ones had to leave behind. Love and life remain within us, and the potential for meaning is always there.

CHAPTER FIFTEEN

Everything Has Changed Forever

If there ever comes a day when we can't be together,
keep me in your heart, I'll stay there forever.

—Winnie the Pooh

My partner, Paul, and I were on an East Coast lecture tour for therapists in three different cities in the Baltimore area. I was teaching about healing grief and Paul was demonstrating grief yoga. That first evening, we went back to the hotel to watch some TV. I was flipping channels and scrolling on my phone to see which restaurants were nearby when I suddenly received a text notification that my older son, Richard, had dialed 911. This wasn't the first time that had happened. Richard, who was then twenty-two, David Jr., who was twenty-one, and I shared the same phone plan, so when one of us called 911, we all knew it. I had called 911 for different reasons over the years. Once I reported a woman on the freeway trying to cross lanes when her car broke down. I often called in a car accident and my boys had learned that they should help others whenever they could. Anytime I was notified that one of my sons had called 911, I would get in touch so he could tell me about whatever he was reporting.

I called Richard, but it went directly to voice mail. Since the boys were very close and usually knew what was going on with the other one, I texted David and left a message saying, "Your brother just called 911. Do you know what's up?"

After a couple of minutes of no response, I continued to flip channels as I tried my older son again. Then I called again. This time I was surprised when David's roommate answered the phone. I was not prepared for what he told me. "David's dead," he said, crying. "Your son's dead."

"David's dead?" I yelled.

Paul jumped up and I turned on the speaker phone. I knew what the words "Your son is dead" meant, but I had to ask: "Are you sure?" I questioned him. "Tell me what's going on. They need to give him CPR right away."

The roommate handed the phone to Richard. "David's dead," he wailed.

"No," I said. Surely he was wrong.

"The paramedics are on the way," Richard said. "We kicked in the door to David's room and it looks like he's been dead for a while."

At that moment the paramedics arrived, and Richard told me he would call me back. I hurriedly called the airlines to get a flight back home but there were no more flights to Los Angeles. There was a flight to Washington, DC, in about an hour, which would connect to one to Los Angeles, but I couldn't get to the airport in time. There was no way to get home that night.

I called Richard again to find out what was happening. I could hear chaos in the background.

"The paramedics are with David," he said.

"How long have they been there?"

"A few minutes."

"Look in there and tell me what they're doing." I had hoped they were doing CPR, but Richard said they were talking on the phone. I knew what that meant. He'd been dead too long to be resuscitated.

"Ask them who they're talking to," I said, fighting panic. I heard Richard ask them and I heard their answer. The city coroner.

What had happened? Did David relapse and overdose? Did he die by suicide?

By the time the coroner arrived to examine David, my son's godmother, Ann Massie, and his godfather, Steve Tyler, were there. The boys' other godmother, Marianne Williamson, was lecturing that night in Los Angeles, so I knew that if I could reach her she might be able to offer some support to Richard. I left multiple messages that I was on the East Coast, something was wrong, and she should call me back as soon as she could. Then I asked Ann to hand the phone to the coroner.

He told me it looked like an accidental overdose. All indications were that David had had a late night, had come home, undressed, gotten into bed, and gone to sleep.

"Everything has changed forever," I told Paul. I could see the fear in his eyes as I called the airlines again and booked the first flight out in the morning.

After they removed David's body, I asked Richard to take everyone to our house. Marianne called as soon as she checked her messages, and when I told her the news, she was devastated. "Where's Richard?" she asked.

"He's heading home," I told her.

"I'm on my way."

I hung up the phone, the hotel room went silent, and I fell to the floor, folded up into a fetal position, and wailed. It was a primal pain that needed releasing. I felt like I had been crushed by a boulder. Paul sat down behind me and rubbed my shoulders. After what seemed like hours of crying, I got up. I was separated from my living son and my other son was dead. I didn't know what to do with myself. "I need to get out of this room," I told Paul.

We got into the car and Paul drove aimlessly along streets that we didn't know. I asked Paul to pull into a gas station. I walked in and bought a pack of cigarettes. I had quit when I became a father close to two decades earlier, but at that moment, I couldn't have cared less about my health. I lit up a cigarette and sat on a patch of grass on a hill in front of the gas station. I started smoking it. After a few puffs, I put out the cigarette. "It's not helping," I told Paul.

We drove back to the hotel. There was nothing to do but to somehow get through the night until we could leave the next morning and go home.

During the following days, the logistics of dealing with what had to be done were agonizing. No father should have to look down at his phone and see that the coroner is calling. I wondered when they would do the autopsy, which was required by law.

When you are drowning in sorrow, meaning becomes a life raft. What kind of meaning is possible when tragedy strikes? Family and friends coming to the house to be with us had meaning for me. Messages of love and support from others had meaning. The question of whether to bury or cremate David also had meaning, because I realized that it would be important for me to have a grave nearby to visit. And then there were the questions about what would be meaningful for David. What should he be buried in? Who would he want at the funeral? I had adopted the boys when they were four and five. It had been a closed adoption, and no one knew the whereabouts of the biological mother or father, so inviting them was not an option. But there were so many people who loved David and had participated in his upbringing. I wanted to make sure they had a chance to say goodbye to him.

Richard, Paul, and I went to the funeral home to make the necessary plans. Everything seemed surreal. I felt like I was moving through thick air, every step requiring an excruciating effort.

We picked out a casket and then had to find a plot for David's grave. We drove to different areas of the cemetery with names like, Vale of Peace, Enduring Faith, and Murmuring Trees. We could almost feel David rolling his eyes. Then we saw a small area on a hill called Comforting Light. Richard and I looked at each other and he said, "That works." I liked it, too. We stopped and looked at an area on the northern section. The funeral director said, "There are four plots available."

Out of the blue, Richard said, "That's perfect. There's space for me, you, David, and Paul."

Paul and I exchanged glances. I had adopted the boys as a single parent and Paul had come into their lives only three years ago. We had known each other before that, but hadn't begun dating until the boys were nearly finished with high school. Richard and David both loved Paul, and I knew he meant a lot to them, but until then I hadn't realized how much. Later I told Paul that he had found a place in my boys' hearts.

"How do you know that?" Paul asked.

"Because my son is willing to spend eternity with you in a cemetery."

He teared up at that thought. However, I knew our relationship might not survive David's death. If I were Paul, sitting in all this pain after just a few years of living together, I would be thinking, "How long do I have to respectfully stay before I can get out?" If he did leave, I wouldn't blame him. I might do the same if I were in his position. Luckily, he stayed. We are still together, and with an even stronger bond because of having shared this tragedy—which is another way of finding meaning after a death.

In a few days, the autopsy was complete, and David's body was sent to the funeral home. The night before the funeral I asked to see him. I needed to see my child, even in death. What had happened was so unbelievable that I felt like seeing him would help me grasp the reality.

A drapery covered the bottom half of the casket, but I could see his face. He looked peaceful. His hair was neater than it ever was in life. As a parent, however, I could see that he had been through a lot.

One of the mortuary staff came in to check in on me. She told me that she had prepared his body. I asked her, "Did you put his shoes on?" I had brought his favorite pair of shoes, black and hard-toed.

"Yes."

"May I see them?" I knew David would want me to make sure, so he could wear his favorite shoes into eternity.

She took great care to remove the drapery from the casket and folded it neatly. Then she opened the bottom half of the lid ever so slowly, revealing the shoes. Those shoes had meaning for David, so they had meaning for me.

I thanked her and said, "You can close it."

She did it slowly and carefully, as if the smallest movement might disrupt David from his sleep. My heart was touched by the extreme gentleness of everyone who handled David at the funeral home. I'm so aware that when we lose a child, everything takes on meaning, in good ways and bad, small and large.

Marianne had returned to her home in New York, but flew back to Los Angeles to conduct the funeral a few days later. Her daughter, my goddaughter India, also came to LA for the funeral, flying in from London. Marianne has presided over many funerals, but few, I think, for someone she was as close to as she was to David. She walked me through everything. I was lost. She knew it. She told me where to sit, what would happen, who would speak and when. Paul chose the music. Richard wanted to speak.

Richard spoke so tenderly about his brother and the life they had shared. At one point he said, "My brother would not want us to grieve today."

I felt eyes on me. I knew in that moment what people thought. I was a grief specialist who had spent decades teaching about the importance of grieving, and here was my older son telling everyone to "skip it."

Later at the house a few people asked me about it, asking me if I was okay with it. I said, "Yes of course. My message to everyone is that we all grieve differently. That is what Richard's grief looked like. That is what he felt honored his brother." He had every right to say what he did. It took nothing away from me or my work.

I was deeply touched by all the people who made the effort to come to the funeral. I wish David could have seen all the love that was expressed for him that day. People showed up in a million other ways, too, including writing wonderful emails about David and posting them on social media. Some of them were from people I had never met but who had read my books or heard one of my lectures. The love and support I received from so many were deeply meaningful—the only meaning I could find at the time.

After the funeral, I thought about David's apartment. Family members often complain that the bereaved aren't willing to get rid of possessions or change anything in the room after a loved one dies. I understood the instinct to try to hold on to the past, to preserve it in amber, but because my son had two roommates, that wasn't an option for me. They needed to have David's room emptied so they could get a new roommate. No one would want to move into a room filled with someone else's possessions.

After cleaning out the room and packing all of David's clothes into the back of my car, I left the clothes there because I wasn't ready to face bringing them into his childhood home to be washed one last time before taking them to Goodwill. But the next day, when I got into the car, I could smell David's scent. There was no way I was washing those clothes yet, and no way I was giving them away yet, either. I clung to them as the physical evidence of my son's life.

In those first weeks after the burial, it felt like my internal GPS was constantly searching for David and couldn't find him. It was as if he was on a trip and it was time for him to show up but he was late. Yet I knew he wasn't coming, and I was in agonizing pain. I sat by his grave and told myself, "This is where he is now," even as I prayed to God, "Please undo this." I didn't know how to make it better. I didn't know how to live with it. At that time, the pain was my meaning, my only meaning. It showed me how much I had loved him.

Two weeks after my son died, a close friend texted me that a mutual coworker of ours whom she had been very close to had died. My initial thought was "No other death matters but my son's," but my heart reminded me that either all deaths matter, or none of them do. I immediately called her and talked about her loss. For years I've entertained the question of which kind of loss is the worst. My answer remains the same. The worst kind of loss is your loss.

When we're in the acute stage of grief, in that raw place after the loss has occurred, it is meaningful to simply be in the grief. I canceled all my upcoming lectures. I didn't know if I could lecture again. How could I ever do a workshop on grief when I was doubting my own words about the possibility of living again after this loss? I wasn't sure I would survive. How could I help others?

Despite all that I knew about grief, I realized I needed help. I had taught people to reach out when they were in need, and now it was my turn. I was wondering whom to call, but the answer came to me through one of those serendipitous connections that so often arise in life. Years before, in 2003, I had been working on the first draft of my second book with Elisabeth Kübler-Ross, *On Grief and Grieving*. After I complete a draft of a book, I often send a few copies out for peer review. It's my way of discovering what problems need to be addressed while there's still time to correct them. One of the people I sent a copy to is a beloved therapist in Los Angeles, Fredda Wasserman, who was working at a well-respected nonprofit organization called Our House, for people in grief. After she reviewed my pages, she invited me to her home. I remember feeling like a new student who was worried. But I knew that she was there to help me make the book better, which she did. I didn't see her again until years later when we were both speakers in a "Grief in the Workplace" conference.

After David died, I received an email from Fredda. She said she was heartbroken for my loss and she was there if I needed anything. It was hard to take it in. "Wow," I thought. "It's impressive that she knows to reach out at the one-month point." I decided to make an appointment to see her for grief counseling.

When I walked into her office, Fredda gestured me over to the client's chair. I reluctantly took a seat. "It must feel like you're sitting in the wrong chair," she said.

"That's exactly what I'm feeling," I told her. "It's so strange. People want to know how the grief expert is dealing with the loss of his own son. I tell them, 'The grief expert didn't lose his son, the father did.'"

She leaned in and said, "I would imagine both are catastrophic losses."

I went to her weekly, even a couple of times biweekly. Our appointments gave my grief a dedicated time and place, which was important to me. It was a way of acknowledging its power. Fredda was able to recognize the father who couldn't stop crying about his son's death, as well as the grief specialist who was reviewing all his recommendations on dealing with death to see if they were still viable, whether they might work for him, too.

One of the things I talked to her about was that moment at the funeral home when I asked to see David's body and to check on his shoes. I'm Jewish, and Jewish custom often dictates a closed casket. But I had needed to have one last look at my son, needed to capture the stark, brutal reality of seeing him in his casket. I had even taken a photo of him there. I had enormous guilt around this and I told her what I had done. I knew she would understand my guilt. Her response was, "You did what you needed to do, and you needed one last look at him. That's what was most important. That was *your* ritual."

I told her that I had never shown that picture to anyone, and I asked her if she would look at it. She said yes. I handed her the picture and she held it ever so gently and looked at it with me. She paused, really taking it in, and said, "Sweet boy. I'm honored you shared it with me."

I sobbed for the rest of the session. She said very little, just let me cry. That was her witnessing my grief.

In my life at that time, I was drowning in the river that I had helped shepherd so many others across. I felt helpless and lost, vulnerable, overwhelmed. I allowed myself to be all those things with Fredda. We reviewed what happened the night of David's death, and the days that followed. We went back in time. I would talk, cry, yell, and Fredda was always there with me during those sessions. It felt like she was as shocked as I was at David's death.

I continued to see Fredda on and off as needed, and I also began going to a support group for bereaved parents called Compassionate Friends. It was strange to be in a group with my own grief books on display a few feet away. No one there knew I was the writer. Now, when people ask me, "What happens when the grief expert's son dies?" I say, "He does exactly what we all do. He goes to grief counseling and support groups, and he looks for meaning."

Broken Heart Syndrome

There is a phenomenon called broken heart syndrome, which is a temporary disruption of your heart's normal pumping function, often brought on by a surge of stress hormones triggered by a serious event, such as the death of a loved one. Experts agree that within hours or sometimes days of the event, our hormones can cause a temporary ballooning of the left ventricle of the heart, which interferes with the capacity of that chamber to pump blood throughout the body. The syndrome was first reported in Japan in 1990, where it was known as "takotsubo cardiomyopathy," because the shape of the left ventricle during this temporary enlargement is similar to that of a *takotsubo*, a pot used in Japan to catch octopuses, and cardiomyopathy is a disease that affects the ability of the heart muscle to pump blood. Women are more likely to have broken heart syndrome, but anyone over fifty-five is at higher risk.

The symptoms of broken heart syndrome are very similar

to those of a heart attack, but they are usually temporary and cause no permanent damage. However, on occasion the disruption of the pumping function is so severe that it can result in death. We often hear about spouses who have been in long marriages who die shortly after the death of their partner. We find it bittersweet, saying that the living spouse died of a broken heart, which is literally the case. This is one of the clearest possible examples of a mind-body connection. In terms of our body, please note only a physician can diagnosis broken heart syndrome versus a heart attack. If you are experiencing chest pain, it could be a sign of a heart attack, so it's important to take it seriously and call 911.

One day after Barbara Bush's funeral, her husband, George H. W. Bush, was hospitalized. I was interviewed in the media by reporters wanting to know if he was suffering from broken heart syndrome. My answer was how could he not have his heart broken after his wife of seventy-three years had died? President Bush recovered, though he died little more than half a year later. Another possible instance of broken heart syndrome, this one fatal, was the death of Debbie Reynolds, the day after her beloved daughter, actress Carrie Fisher, died. Todd Fisher said that his mother did not die of a broken heart. It was her destiny to be with her daughter. He said, "She just left to be with Carrie." His statement was an example of making positive meaning. He did not see his mother as "brokenhearted," but rather having a closeness that transcended even death.

Any extremely stressful event can cause broken heart syndrome, including the death of a pet. The *New England Journal of Medicine* reported on a sixty-one-year-old woman whose dog died. When she showed up at the hospital emergency room with severe chest pain, doctors performed a number of emergency tests and diagnosed her with takotsubo cardiomyopathy.

I never thought I would have broken heart syndrome, but after David died and the funeral was over, I did experience

chest pain. I wondered if it was this syndrome or if I was having a heart attack. My next thought was that I didn't care. If I
had a heart attack in that moment, it meant I could be with my
son David. In a few days, the physical heart pain subsided. The
reality is that most of us do survive, though the emotional pain
will long outlast the physical pain.

How do you mend a broken heart? By connection. Since
we know that human contact and touch can help our blood
pressure go down, it's not a major leap to think that human
connection can and does actually help with broken heart syndrome. Perhaps being witnessed helps us physically as well as
emotionally. Our heart longs for connection. Anyone who is
going through deep grief can tell you that grief affects your
mind, your heart, and your body. Having our pain seen and
seeing the pain in others is a wonderful medicine for our body
and soul. My work with Fredda and the time I spent in grief
groups began my healing. My friends and family were a critical
part of my healing, too.

Meaning through Connection

One of my mantras is: *It's your job to honor your own
grief. No one else can ever understand it.* I've seen how true
that is.

Someone wrote me the loveliest post on Facebook about
David. It touched my heart to realize that my loss had inspired
such sweet words. The next day the same person posted a
photograph that came up in my feed showing an amazing
dessert.

I felt a surge of resentment. It seemed like everybody in the
world was in a different place than I was. Then I realized I had
a choice: I could blame everyone else for not feeling the pain
I felt, or I could feel my own grief without any expectations
about how anyone else should feel. I could have gratitude for
whatever kindness people extended to me, while recognizing

that they could not be expected to share my feelings. This was my tragedy, not theirs. I thought of the Auden poem "Musée des Beaux Arts," about suffering "while someone else is eating or opening a window."

In the first twenty-four hours after David died, there were friends and family who never left our side. They handled everyone's shock including their own. They were there to help with my every need. They saw to it that there was always someone with me because they knew how to be present in a crisis.

The next day the house was filled with more friends and family. Texts, voice mails, and calls poured in. People answered phones and told the callers how we were doing as if we weren't in the room. They knew we didn't have it in us to repeat the story over and over, so they answered questions and gave out our address and told friends they could just drop by.

After a few days, I noticed that people who could be around the deep pain of the first twenty-four hours weren't around much anymore. Other people showed up who would take me for a walk around the block or go for coffee with me. In the weeks that followed, still others asked me out for lunches and dinners. What was happening was something I had talked about in my workshops and lectures—that in times of grief, our friends are like the instruments in an orchestra, which play many different notes to make up a symphony. There are the people who show up immediately when tragedy happens. That may be their note. The ones who show up in the first month help us walk through our darkest valleys. That is their note. The people with whom we can later begin to return to a more normal life play a different note, as do the people who eventually encourage us to talk about the future.

We may resent people for what we see as their inconstancy, but that is how life works. Everyone has something to offer, and they offer it in their own time. The result of all the contributions is a symphony of meaning. We will hear it only if we listen for it. If we shut our ears out of hurt and anger, we will miss it.

The Three P's

As I considered the factors that could help me heal, I remembered the three P's, the mental attributes that according to renowned psychologist Martin Seligman are what shape our views of the world and determine how well we will be able to deal with setbacks:

1. Personalization—whether you attribute an event to internal or external causes, that is, whether you blame yourself for it, or feel like the only one who has ever suffered such a tragic loss.
2. Pervasiveness—the belief that a negative event will destroy everything in your life.
3. Permanence—the belief that the effects of a loss or a disaster will last forever.

When I thought about how I was going to apply the three P's to the loss of my son, I knew I would have to acknowledge, in terms of personalization, that though this loss had happened to me, it was not because of me. And I was not unique in my suffering, either; had not been singled out by God or fate or whatever to undergo this ordeal. I had spent enough time with the brave parents and other survivors of loss I had met in my lectures and retreats to know not to personalize my loss. Many others had experienced something like it, and I had counseled them not to blame themselves. Thinking about this helped me feel less alone in the world and in my loss.

Thinking about the second P, pervasiveness, I knew that my life would not be destroyed by David's death. Nor would my work. Because of the tragedy, my work would if anything become deeper, and perhaps I would grow in wisdom. My heart grew lighter at the thought that David could somehow help me help others. The helper in him could live on in me.

As for the last P, permanence: I knew there would be a permanent hole in my heart, but I also knew that the pain would not last forever. I would change, transform, and become different in ways I could not yet imagine.

Back to "A New Different Normal"

No one likes or wants this new normal. In time I found, as most grievers do, that returning to the activities of daily life was helpful. Even though my world would never be normal again—or not the old normal anyway—my routines helped to stabilize me. Among other decisions I had to make about how I wanted to spend my time, I needed to decide if I would keep canceling lectures or return to work. I knew I had to try, so after a couple of months I started giving my lectures again. My first lecture was in front of a few hundred police personnel who were trained as peer support within the LAPD. Perhaps on a subconscious level I knew they would be a container for my loss. My next talks were makeup lectures for the ones that were canceled when David died. Those were the ones I most feared, because I knew everyone in the room would be aware of what I had just been through and I wasn't sure I could maintain my composure. I began my lecture by thanking everyone for being patient with the cancellation and rebooking. I was holding it together when one woman said, "I was shocked when I received that call that your lecture was canceled because your son died. I have been praying for you every day and thinking of you and your family."

I said, "I felt those thoughts and prayers, they were my cushion. I deeply appreciated it." I truly meant that. It had been healing for me to feel the love of so many people. Many of the comments they made on social media were so touching that I would go back and reread them again and again. Some people wrote directly *to* me. But there is also a strange phenomenon on social media in which people talk to each other about someone else via comments on that person's pages. I would read posts on my page from people who seemed to be having a private conversation *about* me.

"Wait, he was helping someone whose child had died?"

"No, his son."

"David's own son? That can't be. I just heard him at a lecture talking about his sons a few months ago."

"Yes, his son."

"That seems wrong. The grief expert's son dies? That's just heartbreaking."

"What can we do to help?"

All of these thoughts and comments, to me and about me, were so kind, and so meaningful.

The next few lectures were for therapists and counselors. Most of them had not heard the news. It was a balancing act. I knew if I mentioned my loss early on, they would try to help me—and possibly resent it later. No one wants to spend their hard-earned money to come to a lecture on caring for those in grief only to suddenly find themselves taking care of the teacher. I decided I would mention David only at the end of the day. If someone said early on or on a break that they were sorry for my loss, I would thank them but then quickly move forward with the lecture. I saw myself as no different from anyone who goes to a job where they can't just stop their work and start talking about their loss. However, after I had given them the tools or information they came for, I did talk briefly about my own recent experience. I ask people to be open and honest about their losses, so I had to do the same.

When the end of the year came around, I had to face spending the first holiday season without David. It would be a struggle for Richard and for me. As a parent, I wanted the holiday to be good for my older son, but I didn't want to interfere with his grief. In our home, we celebrate both Chanukah and Christmas, so I mustered up the strength to take out the Christmas tree and the Chanukah menorah. My son sat on the couch. I poured him some eggnog and he smiled and took the glass. I told him that I could only do the lights, but I couldn't do the ornaments yet. I began circling the tree with lights and asked him if he wanted to help. He shook his head no.

In the past I would have coaxed him or pretended to have a problem with the lights for him to solve. But I knew better. This was his grief and I wasn't about to try to gloss over it. None of us like it when people, no matter how well intentioned, try to take away our pain before we are ready to let it go. He sat. I hung lights. That was it.

Richard and I went to David's grave a few days before Christmas. After a long period of silence, Richard said, "I'll never enjoy the holidays again."

"I know what you mean," I said. "They'll never be the same without David. But if I'm lucky, I'll be around for twenty to thirty more years. We don't have forever together, and during those years, I hope to spend the holidays with you. I'm always going to miss David and I hate that he will never be with us again. But I would like to think we will be able to celebrate our holidays in the years to come. Of course, that will take time."

Richard looked as if he were picturing year after year in his head. "Yes," he finally said. "I want to enjoy Christmas, too."

"Someday we will."

Making that a goal for the future, while accepting how bad things were now, changed everything. Somehow it added a feeling of hope to the air. And it took the pressure off trying to enjoy Christmas when that seemed impossible. Later Richard and I joined Marianne and her daughter, India, exchanged gifts, and ate a delicious meal that India prepared. We talked, cried, and reminisced with family and friends. We were fully present for the grief we were experiencing, but also aware that we still had lives to live. It's not a holiday I would ever want to live through again, but because of sharing it with friends and family, it was a very meaningful one.

People often say, "I don't know how you're doing it." I tell them that I'm not. I'm not deciding to wake up in the morning. I just do. Then I put one foot in front of the other because there's nothing else to do. Whether I like it or not, my life is continuing, and I have decided to be part of it.

Rebuilding with Meaning

In grief, we are faced with the question of how we will find meaning in the rest of our lives. Though we cannot help thinking that what would be most meaningful would be to have our loved ones back, we know that is not possible. Faced with the reality that we didn't get enough time together, we must ask ourselves, "What would best honor the years they didn't get?" That could be one way of bringing meaning to our lives without them.

People often think there is no way to heal from severe loss. I believe that is not true. You heal when you can remember those who have died with more love than pain, when you find a way to create meaning in your own life in a way that will honor theirs. It requires a decision and a desire to do this, but finding meaning is not extraordinary, it's ordinary. It happens all the time, all over the world.

Before one of my lectures, a participant approached me and said with enthusiasm, "I'm looking forward to hearing you speak. Is this a talk about your son's death?"

"No," I said. "I'll be speaking about helping people who are experiencing grief."

My work is not about my son's death. This book is not about his death. But his death has clearly deepened my work. I want his life to be more than the way he died. Some of the meaning I have found is that life doesn't owe us. We owe it. There are people who walk this earth in awe of the life around them. They are not people who have had a perfect life. The truth is they are often the ones who have had a lot of tragedy. They are not on TV or posting on Facebook or Instagram about how wonderful their life is, they are living it. I know if you're reading this, awe may be a stretch for you, just as it is for me. But if Viktor Frankl and his fellow prisoners could be awestruck while watching a sunset on their way from one concentration camp to another, we have to think that we will be able to find that capacity in ourselves.

There are magical moments to be had with our living loved ones now. Our job is to find them and cherish them. Through them, we can still find a sweetness in the world.

There are challenges to finding meaning. Every moment we are making choices—whether to move toward healing or to stay stuck in pain. Like all the other stages, the sixth stage of grief requires movement. We can't move into the future without leaving the past. We have to say goodbye to the life we had and say yes to the future. My son's death will always be a part of me, and one of my goals is to figure out who I am in this future without him. That is how I will begin to rebuild.

Ask yourself, "Who would I be if I changed and grew with this loss?" More important, who will you be if you don't? I am a grief specialist who tries to make meaning out of the worst moments of our lives. Now that your loved one has died, who are you?

Final Thoughts

After sitting at countless deathbeds, I can tell you, no one pines for their houses or cars at the end of life. What is meaningful is the people whom they have loved.

When I was lecturing in Germany, I visited the city of Hamburg. I knew about World War II and Hitler and the concentration camps. I had even been to Auschwitz and Birkenau. But I didn't know Hamburg's history. When I arrived in Hamburg, I was surprised that everything there looked new. I expect cities in Europe to be old. I asked someone why all the buildings in Hamburg seemed to be new. The answer surprised me.

"The British and Americans bombed it in World War II," I was told, "and the city was destroyed, so it had to be rebuilt from scratch."

I was embarrassed that I didn't know that. I learned that there was only one part of the city that had not been torn down and rebuilt—the church of St. Nikolai in the center of the city, which had been left standing in ruins, exactly as it was the day after the bombing. It is now a memorial to the people who lost their lives in the air raids. The peace garden and sculpture on the grounds attest to the universal longing for peace and reconciliation. When I went to visit the church, I could see that the blackened remains of its beautiful bell tower were forever shrouded in sadness. But there was something surprisingly life-affirming about them, too. They seemed to be a testimonial to continuity and resilience.

I met with Helga, a volunteer there, who said that when she

was five, she watched her parents run from the fire and try to save her. She saw the flames from above engulfing her mother and father, and everywhere she ran, there was nothing but the fiery red of the flames. Someone yelled at her to look for the dark spots, the only places where there was no fire. And then that person, too, disappeared into the red flames. Helga ran from one dark spot to the next, and somehow she survived.

"I'm so sorry," I said after she told her story. I was from the country that dropped the bombs that killed her parents, as well as tens of thousands of others.

"I used to be angry," she said. "But as I matured, I understood that it had to happen that way for the good of the world."

This amazing woman was someone who had moved beyond seeing the death of her parents from the point of view of a child and was now able to understand the terrible history that explained what happened to them. She had become a citizen of the world, and had assumed the responsibilities of citizenship, where she saw herself as part of something larger.

I often think of St. Nikolai church, forever destroyed, sitting in the middle of a beautiful modern city. Then I think about my dear sweet David. There is a part of me that stands just like St. Nikolai, my heart forever devastated by his death. I know that pain and longing will never go away until the day we are reunited. Yet I feel like Hamburg. I have to build something around my devastation.

We often believe that grief will grow smaller in time. It doesn't. We must grow bigger. We must be the architects of our lives after loss. I know that David would not want his death to constrict my life. He would want to expand it. That's what I am trying to do. That is my meaning.

Your heart may be devastated. It may feel like your loved one was the only thing that gave your life meaning. But that meaning lives within you and is always possible to find again. It may feel like all meaning left with the person you lost, but that is not true. You can continue to connect meaningfully with those who are still living, and you can form new connections, too. Those connections do not diminish your love for the person who died. They will only enhance it.

After all my years working with the dying and the grieving, I have found that in this lifetime, the ultimate meaning we find is in everyone we have loved. Your loved one's story is over. For unknown reasons, their time on earth has drawn to a close, but yours continues. I can only invite you to be curious about the rest of the story of your life.

You have most likely struggled with the acceptance of your loved one's death. Perhaps it's time for you to move on to the next stage of grief. Find your meaning. Your future is still unwritten. You have loved, you have experienced great loss, but life continues. Explore that. Be curious about that. You will never be the same, nor would you want to be. You can be whole again, however, and you deserve to be.

When my boys were young, they would ask, "Daddy, do you believe in God?"

My answer was always yes. They would follow up with, "How do you know for sure?"

"Because I found you. There are millions of children in this world, and yet it was the two of you who came into my life. Our getting to be together is the miracle that makes me know God exists."

Now that David is gone, do I think we will all somehow be together again in the next place? I do. How that will work, I have no clue. I know that he has left this realm, but I sense unseen connections that bind soul to soul, and I believe those connections will survive death and unite us in the next realm, whatever and wherever that is.

I always think about the twins in the womb story:

In a mother's womb were two babies. The first baby asked the other: "Do you believe in life after this world?"

The second baby replied, "Why, of course. There has to be something after this world."

"Nonsense," said the first. "There is no life after this world.

What would that life be? The umbilical cord supplies nutrition. Life after this would be impossible. The umbilical cord is too short. There can't be a world after this one."

The second baby held his ground. "I think there is something, and maybe it's different than it is here. Maybe we'll see each other there."

The first baby replied, "If there is another world, no one has ever come back from there. Leaving here is the end of life, and after delivery, there will be nowhere to go and nothing but darkness."

"Well, I don't know," said the twin. "But certainly we'll see Mother and she will take care of us."

"Mother?" The first baby guffawed. "You believe in a mother? An all-powerful, intelligent being that makes all this happen? Where is she now?"

The second baby calmly and patiently tried to explain. "She is all around us. It is in her that we live. Without her, there would not be a world."

"Ha. I don't see her, so it's only logical that she doesn't exist."

To which the other replied, "Sometimes when you're in silence you can hear her, you can perceive her. I believe there is a reality after this world."

That story makes me think that just as an infant before birth could never imagine what life after birth could be like, or even believe it exists, we cannot imagine life after death. I think in some form, some way, I will see my parents, my nephew, and all those who have died before me. And mostly I hope to see my dear son David again. He may know everything that has happened since he died. But maybe not. Maybe he and my mother and others will ask me about the gift of the years that followed their death. What did I do with that gift? What's my story? Did I make the last chapters of my life meaningful? I hope I have something interesting to tell them.

My hope is the same for you. I hope you will have something interesting and meaningful to say about the rest of your life.

Acknowledgments

How do you thank people who helped you after the death of your son? They had the endurance to support me in writing my most personal book to help honor my son and so many others who have died.

This book percolated in my mind for a long time prior to David's death. Finally, I came to realize there was a sixth stage of meaning to help me and others. I am so grateful to Ken Ross and the Elisabeth Kübler-Ross family and Foundation for allowing me permission to add to the iconic five stages of grief.

When I decided to reach out to my agents at WME and share this concept, I was so grateful for Jennifer Rudolph Walsh's encouragement as she connected me with smart and supportive agent Margaret Riley King, who helped make this book a reality.

Simon & Schuster and the Scribner imprint has always been a publishing house, but it became family after David died. I'm so grateful for the tenderness that Nan Graham and Roz Lippel showed me. My editor, Kathy Belden, was a confidante, a shepherd, and a sounding board that every writer deserves and rarely gets. Books like this don't come together without a lot of red ink. Beth Rashbaum was the magician that helped me become the wordsmith I had always hoped to be. Always present was my dear friend and editor, Andrea Cagan. After David died, she sat down at my computer and said, "Let's get some of these words down. You'll want to remember these details later." Her ever-present guidance is a true gift in my books and life.

My writing world can only reflect my personal world. My

son Richard continues to amaze me with his strength and love for David. After many storms, Richard is a true survivor. He is my sixth stage.

I'm deeply grateful to my partner, Paul Denniston, who got more than he ever signed up for. He was my rock during David's death. He lived through the acute grief and then relived it through the agony and healing as I wrote this book. He has remained by my side as an ever-present example of unconditional love.

For decades, Marianne Williamson has been my dear friend and true inspiration. Her courage and compassion have always been remarkable. She was my beacon when my son died.

My deep gratitude to my goddaughter, India. Your brilliance and grounding is always my true north.

There are so many friends and colleagues who deserve my deep thanks for being on the journey of my life and this book. Adele Bass, Annie Gad, Ed Rada, Ann Massie, Jim Thommes, Rachel Hanfling, Rebecca Hammond, Krista Richards, Connie Whelchel, Patrick Allocca, Fredda Wasserman, Ron Spano, Dianne Gray, Jennifer Sindell, Denise Jablonski-Kaye, Steve Tyler, John McCrite, Richard Ayoub, Lee Edmiston, Ella Edmiston, Paulette Forest, Garrick Colwell, Kate Sample, Linda Jackson, Bonnie MacBird, Claire Zelasko, Mark Vierra, Anna Rustick, Dr. Janina Fisher, Beth Segaloff, Marty Majchrowicz, Carmen Carrillo, Rodney Scott, Lita Weissman, Ben Decker, Alana Stewart, Bessel van der Kolk, Deborah Morrissey, Licia Sky, Tally Briggs, Chris Howard, Matthew Lombino, Stephen Roseberry, Nastaran Dibai, Katrina Hodes, Jeffrey Hodes, Liz Hernandez, Byron Katie, Gregory Hoffman, Juan Lopez, Project Angel Food, and the Farrah Fawcett Foundation.

And last but certainly not least, to those in this book who have shared their lives, deaths, and experiences and continue to be my teachers. I am inspired and touched by their love and courage and the meaning they find.

About the Author

David Kessler is the world's foremost expert on grief. His experience with thousands of people on the edge of life and death has taught him the secrets of happiness, even after tragedy. He coauthored *On Grief and Grieving* and *Life Lessons* with Elisabeth Kübler-Ross. On his own, he is the author of *Visions, Trips, and Crowded Rooms* and *The Needs of the Dying*, which received praise from Saint (Mother) Teresa. He also coauthored *You Can Heal Your Heart: Finding Peace After a Breakup, Divorce, or Death* with Louise L. Hay. He has spent most of his life teaching physicians, nurses, counselors, police officers, and first responders as well as working directly with those experiencing grief and trauma. He has volunteered with the American Red Cross, helping after two aviation disasters and 9/11. He is a specialist reserve officer with the LAPD. David is the founder of Grief.com, an invaluable resource to millions who are grieving.